THE AMAZING
BLONDE WOMAN
DIETRICH'S
OWN STYLE

THE AMAZING
BLONDE WOMAN
DIETRICH'S
OWN STYLE

'They fascinate,
They captivate,
Beware . . .
The amazing blonde women'

PATRICK O'CONNOR

BLOOMSBURY

For Cynthia Kee

First published in Great Britain 1991
Bloomsbury Publishing Limited,
2 Soho Square, London W1V 5DE

PICTURE SOURCES
Eve Arnold/Magnum: pages ii, 124, 159
Cecil Beaton courtesy of Sotheby's London: pages 33,
42, 52, 53, 54, 55
BFI Stills, Posters and Designs: pages 26, 30 *middle*,
32 *top* & *bottom left*, 34–5, 36 *bottom left*, 37, 64, 68, 69,
83, 84, 95 *bottom*, 96, 109, 110, 117 *top*, 138 *top*
Camera Press Limited: pages 121, 140, 141
Collection Christophe L: page 90
Hulton-Deutsch Collection: pages 6, 12, 22, 32 *bottom
right*, 36 *top* & *bottom right*, 56, 57, 58, 60 *top*, 65 *top left*
& *right*, 81 *top*, 86 *top*, 89, 92, 93, 94 *top*, 95 *top*, 108,
111, 112, 113, 119 *top right*, *bottom left* & *bottom right*,
120 *bottom right*, 126, 136 *bottom left* & *bottom right*,
138 *bottom*, 139 *bottom*, 142 *bottom*, 151 *top*
Kobal Collection: pages 27, 38–9, 65 *bottom left*, 98,
143, 145 *top left*
Popperfoto: endpapers, pages i, 11, 23, 24 *top*, 28, 72,
97, 118, 119 *top left*, 120 *top right*, 123 *top*, 136 *top*,
137, 144, 145 *top right*, *bottom left* & *bottom right*, 147,
148, 150, 151 *bottom*, 152
Roger-Viollet: pages 81 *bottom*, 82, 94 *bottom*, 146,
149
Topham Picture Source: pages 114 *bottom*, 115, 116,
120 *top left*, 123 *bottom*, 139 *top*, 142 *top*
All other pictures from the author's collection

A CIP catalogue record for this book
is available from the British Library

ISBN 0-7475-1032-6

Designed by Bradbury and Williams
Typeset by Florencetype Limited, Kewstoke, Avon
Printed by Butler and Tanner Limited,
Frome and London

INTRODUCTION

It is a peculiarity of twentieth-century dramatic criticism that the audience is seldom mentioned by reviewers. This was not the case in the last century, when critics were often as interested in who was attending a performance as they were in the events on the stage. Perhaps this contemporary neglect is a legacy of the cinema, and more recently of television and video; private viewing has certainly blunted our perception of ourselves as members of the public.

Marlene Dietrich, who single-mindedly channelled her energy into creating a unique style, always attracted a specialized following. The late J.W. Lambert once suggested that the novels of Ivy Compton Burnett had always been the favoured reading of 'masculine women and effeminate men'. The same could have been said of Dietrich, although when the question was once put to her in an interview by the same Jack Lambert she swept it aside. In her autobiography she insists that 'the roles I have played in films have absolutely nothing to do with what I really am'.

What follows, then, is a celebration of the *public* life that Dietrich turned into an engaging game of hide-and-seek with the press. It does not pretend to be a definitive study of her films, nor an in-depth biography. I was captivated by the Dietrich myth at the age of ten, when I first saw some of her films and heard the records from *The Blue Angel*. It was the writer of the English lyrics for that film who hit upon the happy phrase 'the amazing blonde women' – a label that would endure throughout Dietrich's career.

Thirty years after *The Blue Angel*, Dietrich's presence was still so potent that when Cynthia Kee met her in Paris 'the murmur in the hotel bar froze. Quite suddenly, in a few silent strides, Marlene Dietrich was there. She really is quite something. She was wearing a wild mink coat; a black Balenciaga dress embroidered at the left breast with the scarlet bar of the Légion d'honneur; a stiffened black tulle hat; white kid gloves; black patent leather pumps and a black crocodile handbag. That's all. But the quality of her body gave the mink a luxury no advertiser could ever buy; the black dress was littler and subtler than volumes of *Vogue* could imply, and her single decoration was somehow more worldly and wicked than all the jewellery in Paris, London and New York put together.'

Part of Dietrich's charm has been that she has always succeeded in presenting herself simultaneously as a *femme fatale* and as a friendly, practical *hausfrau*. 'Never confuse movement with action,' was the philosophy that she claimed Hemingway had taught her. Erich Maria Remarque, the other great writer with whom she enjoyed a long friendship, gives a description of the heroine of his novel *Arch of Triumph* that might well be an evocation of Dietrich: 'The high brows, the widest eyes, the mouth – combined to shape a bright, mysterious face – a face whose openness was its secret. It neither hid nor revealed anything. It promised nothing and thereby everything.'

Dietrich has always been a very beautiful woman. The bone structure of her face lent itself to the particular lighting and photography that the cinema of the 1930s and 1940s delighted in; her unerring ability to pose successfully for the camera was evident even in the work of Alfred Eisenstadt – before her discovery by Josef von Sternberg. It was this talent, together with her sense of humour and timing, that kept the Dietrich formula potent long after her contemporaries had resorted to character roles or Grand Guignol in order to prolong their careers.

Dietrich's interest in the technical side of photography (which resulted in her being made an honorary member of the lighting and cameraman's union in Hollywood) meant that she became not only one of the most frequently photographed personalities of the century but also a favourite model. Each photographer paid tribute to her knowledge and control of the medium, even when they did not particularly want to use her favourite overhead and side-lighting – which achieved the shadow under her nose and the sunken cheeks with which she is forever associated. Even now, in the poses of modern stars like Madonna, Boy George and Ute Lemper, one can see the influence of this use of shadow.

Dietrich also paid great attention to fashion. When she was the guest editor of French *Vogue* in December 1973, she defined her interest in clothes thus: 'C'est la silhouette qui compte! J'ai toujours aimé les grands chapeaux, les chaussures claires avec les bas clairs . . . le blouson . . . le blazer . . . les shorts longs avec des talons plats . . . les shorts courts avec les talons hauts . . . les sweaters . . . le cuir . . . les jabots . . . les complets d'homme.' The masculine attire she often wore off-screen in the 1930s, the military uniforms she wore in her role as camp-following entertainer during the war and the blue jeans, cowboy boots and black leather coats she favoured off-stage during her endless tours in the 1950s and 1960s kept the contrast going between her sensual and austere images. In 1960 Dietrich asserted, 'I am not in the least sentimental about clothes. Nothing makes any difference to the way I feel when I am wearing it. I have never felt jealous. I have no favourites among my clothes and there are plenty of people waiting when I have finished with them . . . If I dressed for myself I wouldn't bother at all. Clothes bore me. I'd wear jeans.'

The immense effort that Dietrich put into her image and its preservation was part of her habitual and famous ultra-professionalism. Al 'Whitey' Schafer, director of still photography at Paramount Studios – where many of Dietrich's most famous films were created – wrote, 'Most camera-wise of all my subjects . . . Marlene knows instinctively when a camera angle is right. Usually she is correct. She says she can tell from the amount of heat coming from the lamp. Marlene often edits her own publicity stills and nobody objects because she knows what she's doing.'

John Engstead, who worked with Dietrich for many years – as a still photographer and doing publicity for her appearances in Las Vegas – said that she worked harder than any other subject he had known. This was probably because, as she says nowadays, she was a woman working alone for a lot of her life. Her comment brings to mind the character in her first US film, *Morocco*, who declares, 'There is a Foreign Legion of women, too. But we have no uniforms, no flags, and no medals when we are brave. No wound stripes when we are hurt.' That such a character should choose, in Harold Hobson's words, to celebrate virtue 'not in a sackcloth and ashes but with frankincense and myrrh', and do it with such a good-natured sense of the ridiculous, has been one of Dietrich's most endearing qualities.

There are hundreds of stories about her working with photographers. One that emphasizes Dietrich's remarkable style comes from that apostrophe to the glories of the advertising industry, *The Blackglama Story*. The long-running advertising campaign 'What becomes a Legend most?' had attracted stars of every magnitude, from

Lauren Bacall to Lillian Hellman and Maria Callas. No reply came from Dietrich until the agents delivered a number of mink coats to her apartment in New York. She eventually chose a long coat with a hood for the shoot. In the studio she asked for a full-length mirror, and once the lights were in place she sat on a high stool for twenty minutes arranging the folds of fur this way and that. Finally satisfied, she pulled back the skirt of her gown, crossed the million-dollar legs, looked straight at the camera and said, 'Now!'

1

Lola-Lola

I n the closing pages of *La Fin de Chéri*, Colette describes the young hero's obsession with the past beauty and elegance of his one-time lover, Léa, whom he can no longer see. He visits one of her old friends, and is eager to hear repeated over and over again the details of Léa's great days:

> 'He would listen only to stories without malice in them, and glorifications of a purely descriptive nature. He insisted upon strict respect for documentary truth . . . He stocked his mind with dates, colours, materials, and places, and the names of dressmakers.'

Movie buffs, record collectors and entertainment freaks have exactly the same obsession with the comings and goings, the variant costumes and the unpublished takes of their chosen idols. Was it in Las Vegas that she first wore the silver top hat and tails, or in Rio? The dress in *Monte Carlo Story* is similar to the one she wore on stage in London in 1963, but is not the same.

A ny career that has been as extravagantly documented by the camera – moving and still – as Marlene Dietrich's, leaves itself open to varied interpretations. 'I've been photographed to death and I don't want it any more. *Tempi passat*,' she told Maximilian Schell in his celebrated interview-documentary in 1984.

In the summer of 1973, on the occasion of one of her late appearances on stage in London (which took place at the less than romantic setting of Wimbledon Theatre), Dietrich's unfriendly attitude towards her pet hate, the paparazzi, was openly displayed. The recital, as always, was a wild success. She received a standing ovation and was showered with pink roses by long-haired young men in dinner jackets. Half a dozen photographers rushed down to the front of the orchestra stalls. Dietrich shook her head angrily, grabbed the microphone, and in a tone of command that would have gained her an Oscar nomination, shouted: 'Will the photographers please leave the hall. I sing for the public, not the press. GET OUT.' Once the doors were closed she smiled again and said, 'Now I'll sing another song,' and did 'I Get a Kick Out of You', throwing out her hands to embrace us all on 'You'.

Dietrich's disdain for the 'legend' that was of her own making, and for film writers, biographers and pressmen, is nevertheless at odds with the unstinting effort she always used to put into making a good impression on the public and delivering a professional performance. She always made – and still does make – the headlines, whether she was shooting a film, giving a concert, or simply passing through town. 'Go away, find someone else to talk to,' she said to the reporter who approached her at an airport during that same summer of 1973; her comment and the photograph were on the front page the following day.

Despite her dislike of spontaneous and unposed portraits, during the half-century of Dietrich's public life the press cameramen achieved an interesting and more fragile, less glacial record of her beauty which both complements and contrasts with the studio studies that perpetrated the myth she now so 'detests'.

There can be no legend, no image, without a beginning. Dietrich's origins are well known. Although she used to cloak her age (about which the press harped on endlessly because they liked to call her 'ageless'), when the National Archives in Berlin were made public in 1964 it transpired that she had been born on 27 December 1901. This date is acknowledged in the English translation of her autobiography. Her father, Louis Erich Otto Dietrich, had been an officer in the Uhlan Cavalry; her mother, Wilhelmina Elisabeth Josephine Fesling, was the daughter of a well-known Berlin jewellery manufacturer, whose shop used to be at 20 Unter den Linden. (Sixty years later, Dietrich was to record what remains her favourite LP, *Marlene Singt Berlin*, which includes 'Solang Noch Unter'n Linden' and other 'heavenly lyrics'.) 'Berlin always had something special,' Dietrich said when she was recording this album, 'it was always an island. An island with its special kind of tragic wit without self-pity and without reverence.' She has often insisted that her faults and virtues are German, but that her humour is of Berlin ('The Germans have no humour,' she told Schell). Although nostalgia is an emotion that has been one of the most important factors in the continuation of her fame and popularity – and was central to at least part of her stage performances – she has rejected this idea, claiming that she has fond memories of people, but not of places. 'I've mastered nostalgia,' she said in 1966, 'because I left my country thirty years ago but I have a great nostalgia for the language. I'm sentimental because I'm German, sometimes about the school where I studied music, maybe for a town there, and the fields.'

Dietrich's father died in 1911, and shortly afterwards her mother remarried, to a Colonel von Losch. This has often led to confusion, since Dietrich and her elder sister Elizabeth were sometimes given their stepfather's name. Von Losch died during World War I, at the end of which Dietrich entered the Berlin Hochschule für Musik to study the violin. This tuition was never completed, although Dietrich continued to play the violin, the musical saw and the piano – even if only to amuse others or for a shot in a film. During the terrible years of 1919–21 she somehow found work in the theatre and for a season became a chorus girl in a show staged by Guido Thielscher (a comedian from Berlin once famous for his performances at the Metropol in revues such as *Nacht von Berlin* by Victor Holländer).

The traditions of the Berlin theatre were as rich as they had ever been, despite the deprivations of the Great War and the soaring inflation and economic depression that followed. The satirical revues, great musical comedies, dramas, the innovative stage direction and design, all of which had flourished before 1914, were still to be seen. In later years Dietrich consistently denied that she had had anything to do with the world of Berlin cabaret, and always resented being classified as a cabaret artist. However, as a young performer – whether taking part in the many stage productions with which she is credited, or as a student sampling the theatre of the time – Dietrich was clearly influenced by the richness of the Berlin musical theatre, and its particular sounds can still be heard in recordings made at the time. In his autobiography, Josef von Sternberg describes a meeting he once had with the celebrated film director Max Reinhardt, at which Dietrich was present. She reminded Reinhardt that she had begun her career as a student at his school. His eyebrows, insists von Sternberg, remained raised for several minutes in surprise. Whether this was in shock at the use Dietrich had made of his teachings, or because he could not recognize in the glamorous Hollywood star the student he had once directed, there is no denying that she did act in his theatres, and must have been known to many of his associates.

It is highly unlikely that Dietrich, however famous she later became as a singer, had any musical ambitions in the early 1920s. Her musical career had come to a premature halt through a combination of injury and discouragement from her teachers, so the theatre seemed to offer little enough success at the beginning. She played bit parts in a few movies, and it was on the production of *Die Tragödie der Liebe* that she met her future husband, Rudolf Sieber, who was one of the assistant directors. They married, and in 1926 had a daughter, Maria. Dietrich's struggling career on stage and in films continued; 'I had no career,' she says now, 'I just had a few moments.' Among the plays she appeared in was *Broadway* by George Abbott and Philip Dunning. At first she played a chorus girl, but soon took over the role of Pearl (a part, coincidentally, that was played in a provincial American production of the same play by the young Bette Davis). According to Dietrich, her husband and child never took second place to her career during this period, but talking in 1966 she conceded that Sieber, 'a very, very sensitive person', would never have been able to withstand the life of being in the shadow of a movie star, and said that marriage itself 'has very little chance, because everything speaks against it logically and it's much more difficult for two attractive people to stay faithful. I do think fidelity matters, but that's a woman's point of view.' She went on to say, 'I like the way a man's mind works and I like someone to be master of the house.'

This element of hero-worship seems to have been important throughout Dietrich's career; it coloured all her dealings with her future mentor, Josef von Sternberg, and she certainly idolized Max Reinhardt, even if the 'training' she received from him did not extend beyond taking a few bit parts in his productions. 'There's not much done in the theatre today, and called new, that Reinhardt didn't do first,' she said in 1964. Of all her roles in the 1920s, she later wrote, the 'only one' worth mentioning was Hypatia in Reinhardt's production of George Bernard Shaw's *Misalliance*. If she played this role in the way we can imagine her playing it – knowing what we do of her later acting style – then Reinhardt was indeed a cunning fellow to have assigned it to her at this early stage of her career. The flirtatious daughter of the successful manufacturer is a fairly substantial part which includes the line: 'We get on very well, I think. Nobody else ever called me a glorious young beast. I like that. Glorious young beast expresses exactly what I like to be.' The exasperation this character feels for all the talk that goes on around her is expressed in another line, which also sums up the Dietrich of 1928, 'I haven't had any destiny yet . . . nothing's happened to me. That's why this unending talk is so maddeningly uninteresting to me.'

The English critic David Robinson, writing about Dietrich and her early career at the time of the 1977 Berlin Film Festival Retrospective of her silent films, surmised: 'Able, seemingly, to defy time, Dietrich has perhaps earned the right to deny history.' These stage and film roles of the 1920s, although they were for the most part small roles in big films and larger roles in minor films, at least gave Dietrich the experience that any performer needs.

Although Reinhardt, and later von Sternberg, may have claimed the right to be credited with 'discovering' the best in Dietrich, that honour should really go to the composer Mischa Spoliansky. When Dietrich was auditioning for a part in his revue *Es Liegt in der Luft*, her voice proved unsuitable for the song her fellow hopefuls were attempting, yet Spoliansky took the trouble to play it over in several different keys until he found the one that suited Dietrich's voice. The slyly ironic song about kleptomania is set in a department store, and Dietrich's unmistakable voice can still be heard on the 12″ record of extracts that she and other members of the cast made; it was her recording debut.

Of the Berlin singers of the 1920s whose styles were undoubtedly familiar to Dietrich, and from whom she learned some of her techniques as a *diseuse*, the greatest were Fritzi Massary, Trude Hesterberg, Claire Waldoff and Margo Lion. To this list must also be added the name of Blandine Ebinger, the wife of Friedrich Holländer who was the composer supreme in Dietrich's canon of early songs. It is also important to exclude Lotte Lenya, with whom Dietrich is so often compared; Dietrich can hardly have been aware of Lenya, since the great success of *Die Dreigroschenoper* came roughly at the time when Dietrich was appearing in Spoliansky's two memorable shows. More importantly, the low-voiced style for which Lenya later became famous had not yet developed. In her interview with Charles Higham for his biography of Dietrich, Fritzi Massary maintained that it was Margo Lion more than anyone who influenced the emerging vocal style of Dietrich, and this seems probable when one listens to Lion's most famous record – the 'Tango-ballade' from the French version of *Dreigroschenoper*. Her almost baritone voice (at first one thinks she must be a man) and her wonderful sense of fun were still evident when Margo Lion returned to Berlin in 1978, to give a recital with Mischa Spoliansky at the piano.

On the record that Margo Lion and Dietrich made in 1928, they are accompanied by the wailing of saxophones. (Only six years later these sounds, along with Spoliansky, Dietrich and any number of others from this time, were to be labelled 'degenerate'.) They sing the duet 'Wenn die Beste Freundin', a satire on the Dolly Sisters (the American sisters dance act that was famous all over the world in the twenties); dressed identically in black satin and huge hats, they rivalled each other for the affections of their partner, Oscar Karlweiss. They also imitated the sound of ukuleles, in the fashion of soprano duettists of the time. The bunches of violets pinned to their garments, a reference (that Dietrich claims was lost on her) to the lesbian theme of Edouard Bourdet's play *La Prisonnière*, added spice to the number. It is curious that many survivors of the Berlin of the 1920s have been reluctant to admit the part they played in reinforcing the myth of sexual ambiguity that the city advertised; an element of this ambiguity was part of Dietrich's image right from the start, and she cultivated an androgynous look (even in *Tragödie der Liebe* she is wearing a monocle).

In the issue of *Vogue* that Dietrich edited in the 1970s, she quoted Kenneth Tynan's essay about her, but omitted the following passage:

> She has sex but no particular gender. They say (or at least *I* say) that she was the only woman allowed to attend the annual ball for male trans-vestites in pre-Hitler Berlin. She habitually turned up in top hat, white tie and tails. Seeing two exquisite creatures descending the grand staircase, clad in form-hugging sequins and cascading blonde wigs, she wondered wide-eyed: 'Are you two in love?' '*Fraülein*,' said one of them frostily, 'we are not lesbians.' This Marlene lives in a sexual no man's land – and no woman's either. She dedicates herself to looking, rather than to being sexy. The art is in the seeming.

This idea proved shocking to Dietrich; even in her sixties she was still, as she describes herself, a well-brought up girl of a good family.

Dietrich's next role on stage was in Georg Kaiser's *Zwei Krawatten*, with music again by Mischa Spoliansky. The stars of this show were two great Berlin performers: Rosa Valetti (who the previous season had created the role of Frau Peachum in Brecht and Weill's *Die Dreigroschenoper*) and Hans Albers, with whom Dietrich had already appeared – in a movie called *Prinzessin Olala*. Kaiser's show was set on board a transatlantic liner, and it gave Dietrich – in the words of Alexander Walker – a chance to display 'by turns, flirtatiousness, world-weariness, irony and cynicism'. It opened on 5 September 1929 at the Theater in der Charlottenstrasse. Valetti and Albers had already been engaged to appear in a film, an adaptation of Heinrich Mann's novel *Professor Unraut*, which was the first important 'talkie' to be made in Germany. The film was to be *The Blue Angel*, and the director was the well-known Austro-American, Josef von Sternberg. For the role of the cabaret artiste, Lola-Lola, von Sternberg had wanted Brigitte Helm, but she was unavailable; UFA wanted Lucie Mannheim. However, when von Sternberg came to the theatre to see his other stars, he beheld Dietrich for the first time: 'She had wrapped herself up as if to conceal every part of her body. [Dietrich's costume in the opening deck scene was a heavy travelling coat and hat trimmed with wide bands of leopardskin.] There was an impressive poise about her (not natural, as it turned out, for she was an exuberant bubbler when not restrained) that made me certain that she would lend a classic stature to the turmoil the woman of my film would have to create.'

That night von Sternberg chose Dietrich for the role that was to make her famous; but he still had to convince the studio's casting department, which had already rejected her not only for the role of Lola-Lola, but also, in the previous year, for the part of Lulu in Pabst's film of Wedekind's *Pandora's Box* (subsequently played to such sensational effect by Louise Brooks). It was Brooks herself, in one of the essays she wrote in the 1960s, who defined quite unromantically what it was von Sternberg achieved with Dietrich: 'He could take the most gauche, awkward, sexless dame and turn her into a dynamo of sex . . . If you ever saw her in those pre-Sternberg films, she was just a galloping cow, dynamic, so full of energy and awkward, oh, just dreadful, and the first time he saw her [she was] leaning against the scenery, very bored, because she was working in a play, *Zwei Krawatten*, and didn't give a damn. And he saw that and it was lovely. But all of her movements were horrible. So he simply cut out the movements and painted her on the screen in beautiful, striking poses.'

Von Sternberg requested that Dietrich prepare a song to perform at the screen test. In her recollection of this momentous occasion, Dietrich always claimed that he asked her to bring 'a very naughty song, but I was so sure I wouldn't get the part that I didn't bring the song'. Von Sternberg denies this part of the story: 'It is impossible that I ever asked anyone to be vulgar.' He sent for a spangled costume, into which he pinned her so that it was skin-tight. She perched on top of the upright piano, and the scene technicians blew smoke around. Since she had not brought along a naughty song, they asked her whether she could at least sing some song that she knew. She chose a number by Hugo Hirsch, 'Wer Wird Denn Weinen, Wenn Man Auseinandergeht' ('There'll Be No Crying When We Say Goodbye'). She got down off the piano to demonstrate to the keyboard-player how it went. Von Sternberg said that that was exactly what he wanted and shot the test; the next day all the studio officials said they still wanted Lucie Mannheim.

The decision was left in the end to von Sternberg, who chose Dietrich for the role. He also engaged the musician that Lucie Mannheim, 'a charming, witty young woman', had brought with her; his name was Friedrich Holländer. This talented songwriter was to compose for Dietrich not only the four numbers in *The Blue Angel*, but also – when they were both emigrés in the USA – songs for some of her most famous films: *Desire*, *Destry Rides Again*, *Seven Sinners* and *A Foreign Affair*. Holländer had been one of the resident musicians in the most famous of all the artistic Berlin cabarets, 'Schall und Rauch' ('Noise and Smoke'). There he had composed numbers such as 'Mélodie Perverse', 'Die Kinoduse' and 'General, General' (a warning to all Generals not to start their nonsense again – a call that all too soon was to go unheeded). These and other songs were recorded in the 1960s by Holländer's wife, Blandine Ebinger, and a group of other survivors from the 1920s, including Trude Hesterberg, Valeska Gert and Margo Lion (who were dubbed 'Die Damen von der alten Schule'), and the recordings are instructive when compared with Dietrich's style. One hears immediately that the art of the Berlin *diseuse* was a recognizable tradition from which Dietrich took her method: speaking the words slightly against the music, only singing on the note when it was exactly within her limited range.

By von Sternberg's own admission, his naming of the character Lola-Lola was a tangential reference to Wedekind's Lulu, just as the Heinrich Mann novel on which the film is based is an ironic response to the Lulu plays. In Holländer's song 'Ich Bin von Kopf bis Fuss auf Liebe Eingestellt' (which is somewhat sweetened in its English translation, 'Falling in love again') Dietrich and Lola-Lola become one. As she was being directed in this role, Dietrich complained that she would never again be able to show her face in Berlin, so lewd and shocking were the things she had to do. The downfall of the *petit-bourgeois* professor at the hands of the cabaret artiste is a moral tale, and it is doubtful that a modern audience would be very taken with the idea of the professor's losing out entirely when he exchanges the classroom for the dressing-room. As Andrew Sarris wrote, 'If "serious" criticism of the cinema were not as puritanical as it is, the experiences of Lola and the professor would seem more pertinent to the hidden world of domestic sexuality than is now the case. The idea that all eroticism is hopelessly exotic has made Sternbergian cinema seem much stranger than it is.'

Nevertheless, for the last sixty years audiences have been enthralled by the qualities that von Sternberg could see. He later remarked, 'I did not endow her with a personality that was not her own; one sees what one wants to see and I gave her nothing that she did not have already. What I did was to dramatize her attributes and make them visible.' However, the big shots at UFA in Berlin still could not see her worth, and they announced after the film was completed that they would not be taking up the option on Dietrich's contract. Von Sternberg had returned to Hollywood and called for her to come to the USA. She attended the first night of *The Blue Angel* in Berlin and sailed for the States the next day.

WENN DIE BESTE FREUNDIN

Mischa Spoliansky's revue *Es Liegt in der Luft* gave the Berliners of the late 1920s a first glimpse of Dietrich's fully-fledged personality, if not yet her complete glamour. With Margo Lion and Oskar Karlweis, *below right*, she sang 'Wenn die beste Freundin', a song containing layers of dubious innuendo and sexual ambiguity. It became her very first gramophone hit. The following year Dietrich had a starring role alongside Harry Liedtke in Robert Land's *Ich Küsse Ihre Hand, Madame*. This film is forgotten now, except for the title song by Ralph Erwin, which was recorded for the soundtrack by Richard Tauber (even though it was a silent film). Dietrich demonstrates the art of the hand kiss with Liedtke and Tauber, *above right*.
Left: Dietrich in Georg Kaiser's *Zwei Krawatten*, 1929.

FALLING IN LOVE AGAIN
(CAN'T HELP IT)
WORDS & MUSIC BY *FREDERICH HOLLANDER*

Emil Jannings
in
The Blue Angel
with
Marlene Dietrich

Directed by
Josef von Sternberg
AN UFA PICTURE

A Paramount Release

Famous Music
CORPORATION

THE INEVITABLE ONE

A very large part of Dietrich's success in *The Blue Angel*, *left*, was due to her singing of Friedrich Holländer's songs. As the songsheet demonstrates, the film was originally sold on the basis of its starring role for Emil Jannings. Although von Sternberg denied that he wanted the actresses auditioning for the role of Lola-Lola to sing a 'naughty' song, it was this very quality, the innuendo beneath the rather sugary lyrics (provided by Robert Liebmann), that made the songs – especially 'Ich bin von Kopf bis Fuss auf Liebe eingestellt' – so popular. Dietrich said that she had originally wanted to sing the song 'quite differently, sentimental with lots of German soul. But not at all, he showed me how to sing it. At the time I thought the film was awful and vulgar and I was shocked at the whole thing.' When her famous first recording of it was issued, the 'B' side was 'Blonde Women', the only one of the four numbers that Dietrich did not include in her *tour de chant* in the 1960s. Strangely, very few other singers have ever attempted 'Falling in Love Again'; one of the few was Leontyne Price, accompanied by André Previn, but the rigid 3/4 time that they adopted destroyed the casual charm the number required. The Lola-Lola postcard, *right*, a key element in the film's plot, when the old professor is forced into hawking it, has lost a few of its feathers over the decades.

Lola Lola

No Trilby She

oth von Sternberg, *left*, and
ietrich rejected the Svengali –
rilby label that their
ollaboration was so often
tuck with. If anything, Dietrich
aintained it was more like that
f Eliza Doolittle and Professor
iggins. Von Sternberg
ommented on her tremendous
nergy and her ability to absorb
his direction: 'She was a
perfect medium.' The costumes
were designed by a Hungarian
artist by the name of Varady,
who went uncredited; however,
the series of erotic outfits that
he created for Dietrich *below*,
with Conrad Veidt at UFA, as
Lola-Lola not only established
the personality of the
character's performing style but
led to innumerable echoes
down the years – in Dietrich's
own theatrical wardrobe as well
as in hundreds of parodies.

The film director, wrote von
Sternberg 'is an audience of
one, he controls the camera
according to his vision . . . my
word was law, I was boss.'
Dietrich inscribed a portrait to
him 'Ich bin nichts ohne Dich'
(I am nothing without you).
He wrote sardonically that this
was an accolade he had no
wish to accept, but that 'I must
accept some of the
responsibility for her image in
my films'.

49

In his memoirs Josef von Sternberg claimed that he had never met such a beautiful woman who had been so thoroughly 'discounted and undervalued'. Although she was well dressed, he thought that all the photographs he had seen, including those she valued, made her appear like a female impersonator. Though clearly an exaggeration, the transformation wrought by von Sternberg and the make-up, lighting and hairdressing departments provides ample scope for before-and-after comparisons. *Left:* Dietrich with Fritz Kortner in 1929. All the familiar attributes are present, although the plump face refuses to show its bone structure and the hair doesn't shine. Five years later, *right*, Dietrich seems younger, slimmer and more confident; despite the standard assertion that von Sternberg's transformation makes her seem glacial, in the later portrait she seems warmer. 'I did not endow her with a personality that was not her own,' he wrote. 'One sees what one wants to see and I gave her nothing that she did not already have.'

PERFECTING THE IMAGE

The image of Dietrich that was created through the six films she made with von Sternberg in Hollywood was a process of gradually hardening the sculptural contours of her face, accentuating the cheek-bones, lighting her forehead to give a less rotund shape to the mask and, above all, changing the shape and situation of her eyebrows. From the natural, soft line in the early studio portrait, *this page, top*, taken during the making of *Morocco*, the eyebrows were first strengthened for *Dishonored*, then plucked and sent upwards at an angle for *Shanghai Express* and *Blonde Venus*; for *The Scarlet Empress* they were reduced to the merest pencil line until, in the final scene of *The Devil is a Woman*, the huge 180° arc established that look of permanent astonishment with which Dietrich would coax either fear or laughter.

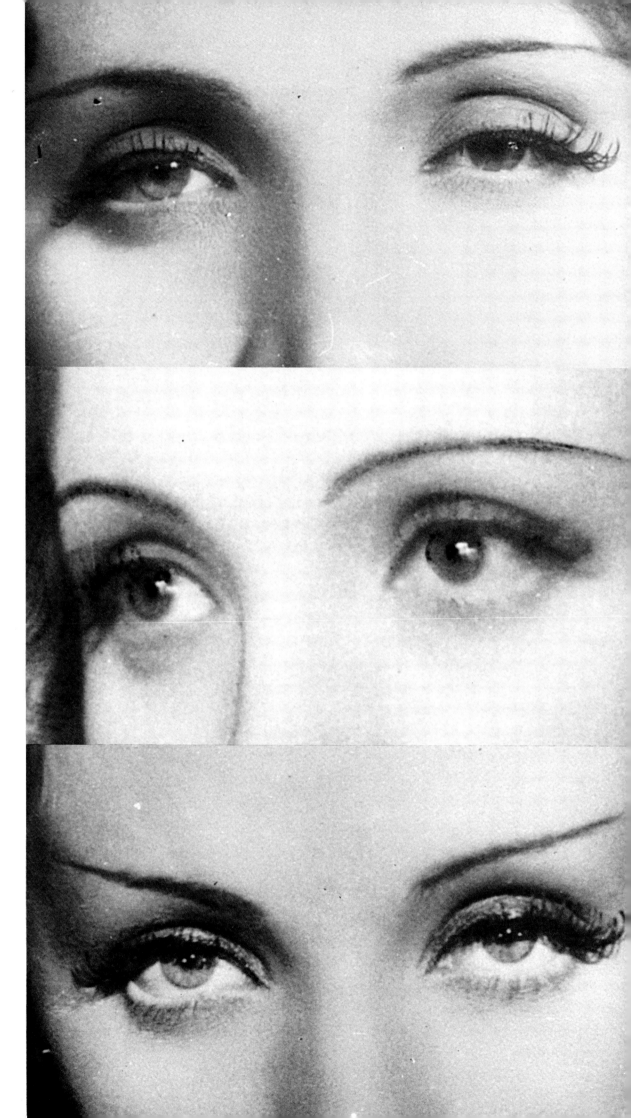

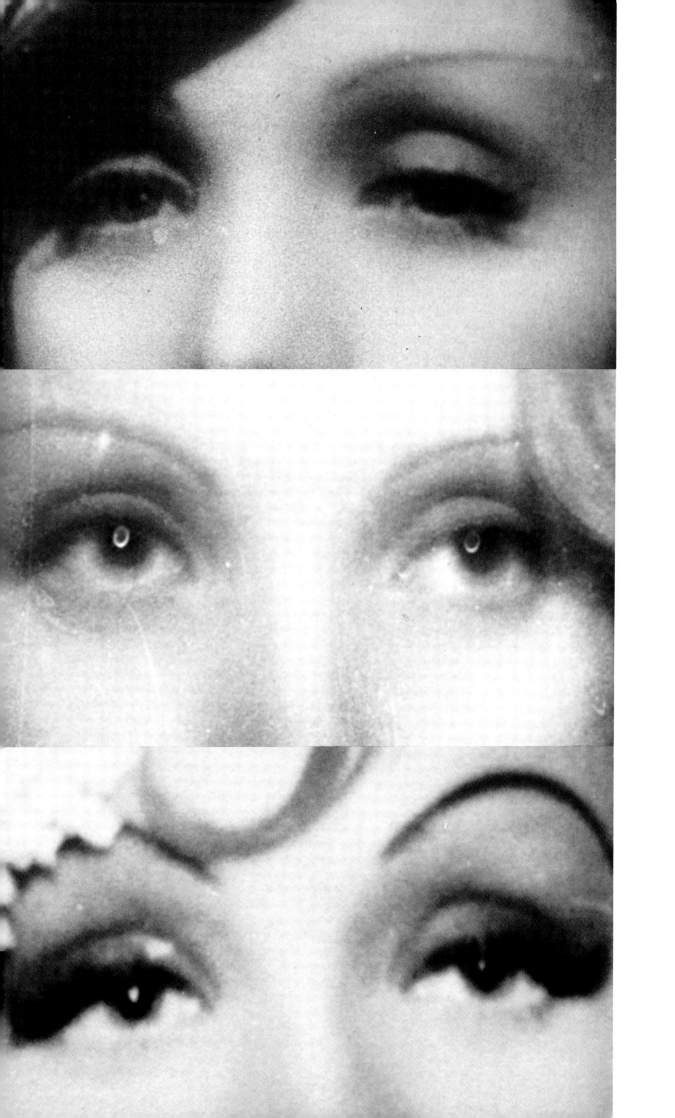

THE ART OF THE TWEEZER

Forty years separate the earliest and the last pictures here, showing the way Dietrich changed the line of her brows to suit the fashion or the role she was playing. All pretence at reality having been abandoned in the mid-1930s, Dietrich allowed her eyebrows to grow again and have a more natural look during World War II. For her role in *Golden Earrings* they were thickened to an almost masculine darkness, then in the 1950s, 1960s and 1970s the altering demands of modern make-up kept the kaleidoscopic eyebrows on the move. From the photograph taken at her dressing-table on the set of *Blonde Venus* to the stark snapshot of her European tour in 1975, the eyebrows are a constant apostrophe on the blank page of her brow; in the 1936 portrait by Cecil Beaton he has mischievously pencilled Dietrich-style eyebrows on to the Roman plaster head.

STUDIO EMBLEM

Mr and Mrs Rudolf Sieber, posing in front of the Paramount emblem at the entrance to one of the studio lots. The oversize fur collar, head-hugging hat, tightly clutched gloves and sensible-length skirt are all typical of the transition phase between 1920s and 1930s fashion. They also reflect the unease with which the studio publicity department dealt with a thirty-year-old married newcomer with a five-year-old daughter. No one in the USA had seen *The Blue Angel* when Dietrich was signed by the studio to make her first American film. Von Sternberg claimed that she left for Hollywood still believing that the film had ruined her, but she cabled him from the boat, 'Who is to play opposite me?'

LEG SHOW

The amount of publicity and the way in which the movie writers of the 1930s concentrated on Dietrich's legs have exaggerated to a tremendous degree the importance they played in her films, although they were used to advantage in *Destry Rides Again*, *left*. Nevertheless, their excellent proportions, which had gained her a place in the chorus-line of several Berlin shows in the 1920s, remained an essential part of the style she projected. The famous still from *The Blue Angel* found its echo down the years, whether in her posing on the set of *Dishonored*, 1931, or playing up to the crowd after her first performance in Sydney in 1966. For her last old-style glamour part in Hollywood, the costume designers found it necessary to decorate her hose with arrows and butterflies.

THE CITY OF LIGHT

On her first visit back to Europe after the success of *Morocco*, Dietrich was snapped in her carriage on arrival in Paris. The suave style (suave, she later declared, was a redundant word) that would make her off-screen image largely indistinguishable from her studio portraits had not yet emerged; here, smiling sweetly, she seems less the *femme fatale* and more the young lady of the house. Her affection for

Paris was to grow from this time on, and she took up residence there permanently in 1960. No one bothered her in Paris, she insisted. They would just say, 'Bonjour, Madame Marlène,' and let her go about her business. After World War II she made it a rule never, never to sing 'Lili Marlene' in France. A song so indelibly associated with the Occupation could bring only bad thoughts with it, she maintained, and if only one person in the audience were reminded of the dark times, then it was worth leaving it out. In Berlin she recorded the French waltz with

which her role in *Morocco* is so bound up, 'Quand l'Amour Meurt'. This was her first recording in French, a song with associations stretching back to the 1900s and to its creator, Paulette Darty, who was known as 'La Reine des Valses Lentes'. This song also features in several other films, notably René Clair's *Le Silence est d'Or* and *Le Petit Théâtre de Jean Renoir*.

An early portrait taken in Hollywood in 1930: Dietrich in costume for *Morocco*.

2

THE
FOREIGN
LEGION OF
WOMEN

The six films that Dietrich and Josef von Sternberg made together in the United States, *Morocco*, *Dishonored*, *Shanghai Express*, *Blonde Venus*, *Scarlet Empress* and *The Devil is a Woman*, form one of the most extraordinary bodies of work ever to have emerged from the Hollywood studio system. The only comparable achievement was the group of films that Garbo made that were photographed by the same cameraman, William Daniels. However, they have none of the cohesion or fascination for movie analysts that the Dietrich-Sternberg films possess, because Garbo's films are the work of many different directors, and are saddled in many cases with over-wordy, pretentious scripts.

It comes as something of a shock nowadays to find deconstructionist – frequently feminist – film historians analysing the *verbal* content of von Sternberg's films. When Peter Bogdanovich asked him about the first of these American films, *Morocco*, quizzing him in particular about Dietrich's appearing in male attire, von Sternberg replied, 'I don't know.' And to a question about whether this scene was abstract, 'They are all abstract.' It is therefore futile to spend too much time analysing the dialogue to work out the formula that proved so enduring. (However, this formula was also a time-bomb, because their 1930s films – after *Shanghai Express* – were not successful at the box office.)

When she was given the opportunity to choose her favourite scenes from her films, first in a season she presented at the Museum of Modern Art in New York, and later in the documentary she made with Maximilian Schell, Dietrich was keen to show how much movement there had been in the von Sternberg films; she also concentrated on the most interesting visual scenes. 'Film . . . MOTION picture,' she tells Schell, before introducing the scene from *Morocco* that was to become such a legend, and which in effect created her first and greatest success in the United States: in top hat, tails and white tie, smoking a cigarette, Dietrich leans nonchalantly against the balustrade of the seedy Moroccan night-club. Oblivious of the audience, whether they applaud or boo, she croons the little slow waltz, 'Quand l'Amour Meurt',

> Lorsque tout est fini
> Quand se meurt votre beau rêve

When she has finished the song, the host at a nearby table offers her a glass of champagne. Draining it in one gulp, she eyes one of his female companions, and asking 'May I have this?' takes a flower from the girl's corsage, leans over and kisses her on the lips. Her subsequent flirtation with Gary Cooper, dressed in his legionnaire's uniform, poses a fascinating triple layer of provocative sexual innuendo. It has to be assumed that this innuendo went unnoticed by prudish audiences and censors (who during the next two years complained of the 'lewd' dialogue and implications in Mae West's films, which were made by the same company, Paramount); the sexual overtones were also the very reason for Dietrich's wild popularity with generations of intellectual and decadent writers and artists.

In 1948, after he had had the unusual experience of meeting Dietrich at his hotel in the early evening, and then seeing Garbo walk through the restaurant while he was dining with Nathalie Paley, Jean Cocteau wrote: 'En quelques minutes, j'ai vu ces trois dames qui représentent toute une époque de ma vie.' Poets, novelists and designers of all nationalities were enchanted by the abstract and erotic world that von Sternberg created around his image of Dietrich. 'I didn't know what erotic meant,' Dietrich says. 'I still don't really know.' Yet the technique adopted by these two geniuses of the screen – for it was an equal match, no matter how much modern film critics brought up on the *auteur* theory like to denigrate the contribution made by the performer – created an image and a style that has proved more durable in its potency than any other similar collaboration (although in later decades the partnership of Arletty and Carné, and Moreau and Truffaut came close).

The arrogance of the Dietrich screen persona in *Morocco*, as represented in the cabaret scene, is offset in the film's opening sequence by the comparative passivity of her rejection of Adolphe Menjou – the debonair man of the world – on the deck of the ship. What is more, she appears to be emotionally wounded when at first she repulses Tom Brown's advances, and also once he has left her, after scrawling 'I changed my mind' in greasepaint over her dressing-room mirror. Part of the Dietrich legend is contained in the first line: 'I don't need any help.' Von Sternberg in his memoirs suggests that she had great difficulty in saying the word help: 'Each time in went the word "help", out came vowels, consonants, and an occasional diphthong that failed to meet any known standard of charm.' The scene was rehearsed and reshot many times: 'On that foul day my reputation as one of the swiftest directors in films was dealt quite a blow.' In the end, by having Dietrich just pronounce the letters h-e-l-p he got the effect he wanted, and it seems quite natural in the film. Curiously, only a few weeks before shooting this scene she had successfully recorded, in English,

> Falling in love again
> Never wanted to, what am I to do?
> I can't help it.

It is therefore hard to understand why she experienced such difficulty with this word in front of the camera. Such stories go towards making a mystery of the quite ordinary craft of film-making, and Dietrich confirms the truth of the story to this day, adding that she burst into tears in her dressing-room afterwards. In another scene she has to leave the room to go and sing. 'Wait for me,' she says as she exits, having paused for what in the final take had to be a count of twenty to achieve the effect von Sternberg desired. Such pacing was only possible, perhaps only desirable, because Dietrich's training and instincts were those of a musician; she was also someone with, in von Sternberg's words, 'the theatre in her blood, and she was familiar with every parasite in it'.

The Dietrich-von Sternberg films all seem to be infused with music, even when – as in *Shanghai Express* – there is none. If *Morocco*, the shortest and gentlest, could be termed a barcarolle, *The Devil is a Woman*, since it is based on Rimski-Korsakov's 'Capriccio Espagnole', must be a capriccio, and *Dishonored*, overlaid from the first moment with talk of death and honour, is a largo funèbre. The sense of music in the film is achieved through wonderful pacing and the different uses made by von Sternberg of slow dissolves, overlapping exposure, conversation and music coming from off-screen in other rooms. Particularly effective is the series of flashbacks used in their final collaboration, *The Devil is a Woman*; these are summoned as if by a stroke of the wand, in jump-cuts.

If *Morocco* had contained the seeds of it – in her contrasted behaviour when *en travestie*, and in her dealings with her suitors – *Dishonored* was to develop further what could be described as the Dietrich 'volte-face' technique; this is the basis for much of her most effective acting, both on-screen and later in her stage perform-ances. This technique was used much more obviously in Dietrich's later films, where the dramatic dénouement usually involves her in a scene in which she suddenly switches from being soft and feminine to being hard and brassy, or sometimes, less effectively, the other way around: the hitherto bold creature (be it Frenchy, Christine Vole or even – in the penultimate moment of the movie – Tanya in Welles's *Touch of Evil*) suddenly turns soft. Nevertheless, the vivid duality of the Dietrich character is present in all the von Sternberg films.

X 27, as *Dishonored* was called in Europe (and the title von Sternberg preferred), like *Morocco* presents an independent Dietrich character. Just as Amy Jolly, the heroine of *Morocco*, declares herself to belong to the 'Foreign Legion of women' who have been wounded and who withdraw from one life to search for some kind of freedom in another, so the street-walker in *X 27* says in the opening scene that she is not afraid of life or death; this is a key part of the Dietrich style.

When asked recently if she thought about death or was afraid of it, Dietrich's reply was no to both questions, and remarked that it is 'more sensible to be afraid of life, but not of death'. The character in *Dishonored* betrays her country as if on a whim, for a man she hardly knows, and then, on trial for her life, answers her judges by murmuring, 'Perhaps I loved him.' She then drives the young lieutenant into a frenzy of pacifist rage: refusing to give the order to fire, he throws down his sword shouting, 'I will not kill a woman.' While the squad waits for his replacement, *X 27* reapplies her lipstick and adjusts her stocking. 'I remember thinking, Oh God, this is awful, what kitsch,' says Dietrich of this scene. Yet her on-screen coolness, which reduces each of her 'sensitive' leading men to rubble, is part of the ongoing attraction that icy, unemotional females hold for audiences. Her scriptwriters played on this appeal, and her personality responded to their demands through good, bad and unbelievable films. If, as von Sternberg insisted, all his films are abstract, it could be argued that not one of Dietrich's films is in any way realistic. Viewed in this light, even those that seem on the surface to have been written as straightforward dramas or comedies, become immediately much more enjoyable as pieces of symbolism.

After their first two films, von Sternberg said he had no wish to continue with Dietrich. 'I was finished. But Miss Dietrich said to me, "You want to show the world you're a great director and that I am a bad actress. Isn't that what you want to do? You want me to go to another director." Unfortunately, being a gentleman, I continued.' What the world would have lost, had they not continued together, were their most highly stylized and – in their day – least popular works. Von Sternberg said that there were no 'fifth-rate stars' – it all depended on how the actor or actress was directed. Dietrich completely agreed with this sentiment: 'I'm an obedient actress. I do exactly as a director tells me.' But for von Sternberg she might never have realized the full potential of her own, highly personal style of performing. He himself said in 1963, 'There are great personalities, and these personalities will break through whatever a director does, or does not, do.'

The 'Dietrich character' was well established after von Sternberg's first two American films: the woman alone, whose past will not let her be at peace, who marches on despite some great hurt and who is still optimistic when she runs fatefully into 'the' man. Von Sternberg cast Dietrich next in a film in which there is no explanation of the heroine's past. As the lady in raven feathers in *Shanghai Express* – who says bluntly when asked if she is married, 'It took more than one man to change my name to Shanghai Lily,' – Dietrich is also allowed to display humour in a slightly bitchy exchange of pleasantries with one of the other passengers, who tries to interest her in her 'boarding house'. As Carol Zucker comments in *The Idea of the Image*, her detailed analysis of the von Sternberg-Dietrich films: 'Dietrich's performance has the precise timing of a great comedienne . . . Her gestures, eye movements and facial expressions are crisper and more definite.'

It is highly probable that Paramount at first saw Dietrich as the woman in their roster of stars most likely to rival MGM's Garbo, who in the early 1930s was still

47

officially the 'greatest star' in Hollywood. There are so many small details that indicate this: Dietrich's entrance in *Morocco* carrying a suitcase, like Garbo's first incarnation in *Anna Christie*; the spy role in *X 27* is a direct reflection of Garbo's impersonation of Mata Hari; and *Shanghai Express*, in which a group of people are thrown together by fate when the train is halted, is an all-star package similar to MGM's *Grand Hotel*. As the Depression began to be felt in every part of American life, for a time it seemed logical to place Hollywood's glamorous stars in a modern, 'realistic' setting: Garbo as the girl on the run in *Susan Lenox: Her Fall and Rise*, and Dietrich as the wife and mother in *Blonde Venus*. For both von Sternberg and Dietrich this was the least important of their films, but it does contain one of the most famous transformation scenes in cinema – when Dietrich emerges from a gorilla suit to sing 'Hot Voodoo' – and also the first instance in their films of her complete volte-face. Once the mother and respectable wife figure has been reduced to a drunken street-walker – last seen in a southern flop-house – a montage of shots of the sea, a restaurant and a cabaret's twinkling lights gives way to the transformation, and there she stands, in white tail-coat and silver topper, singing (in English and French) 'I Couldn't Be Annoyed'.

For modern feminist critics there is a sense of recognition in watching this 'liberated' Dietrich character, who has rejected her rich lover and been rejected by her puritanical husband. ('I hate Women's Lib,' she says now. 'It's just penis envy. They're not women, I call them females. It's very nice to be a woman.') Nevertheless, this trousered Dietrich became, for the 1930s, not only a cinematic marvel, but such an icon of fashion that the Chief of Police in Paris, when she visited the city in 1932, took the opportunity to try and ban her from wearing trousers in public. Dietrich herself denies that she had any influence in this direction: 'I used to wear them when I first came to Hollywood,' she told Elizabeth Dickson in 1966, 'they made sense for our athletic life, tennis and so on and for getting out of low cars.'

The masculine element of her on-screen image adds to the tension that is so noticeable between her and the more aggressive of her leading men (unlike the boy in *Dishonored*, who is immediately reduced to a tearful child). Von Sternberg, as well as the scriptwriters for so many of her later films, always included either a scene in which she is physically assaulted by a man, or one in which her flirtation with the leading man has some kind of violent undertone: Jannings attempts to strangle her in *Blue Angel*; X 27 is shot in *Dishonored*; in *Desire* Gary Cooper asks her if she is still in pain when he has chastised her; and in *Scarlet Empress* John Lodge encourages the young Catherine to strike him with a riding crop. Naturally, the female character always wins this trial of strength emotionally, even if she is left sprawling on the floor at the end of the scene. 'You've got a masochistic complex, dear,' Dietrich assures Maximilian Schell when he attempts to analyse such moments in their documentary collaboration.

Between *Blonde Venus* and the final two films with von Sternberg, Dietrich appeared in Rouben Mamoulian's *Song of Songs*. If the studio had wanted her to attempt to move away from her established image, it is hard to imagine how they thought she might have achieved it in this film. It is enjoyable today chiefly for the last scenes, in which the sweetly demure girl of the early part of the film has once again been transformed by her experiences into a black-feather bedecked cabaret singer, intoning (in English) Friedrich Holländer's 'Johnny'. (Perhaps her demolition of the life-size plaster nude statue could be taken as a symbolic gesture to break out from the image that was being imposed upon her.)

The final von Sternberg-Dietrich films, *Scarlet Empress* and *The Devil is a Woman*, were unsuccessful at the box office. (Because of the way in which the Spanish Army was depicted in the latter film, the pre-civil war government of Spain succeeded in having it banned.) Nevertheless, these two films are the most extreme examples of von Sternberg's abstract technique. *Scarlet Empress* is a symphony in images of sculpture, distorted icons and stylized costumes; the rise of Catherine the Great is played as if in a nightmare infused with images of torture. *The Devil is a Woman* is Dietrich's own favourite among her films 'because I looked more beautiful in that than in any other'. It is also noteworthy for its wonderful use of light and editing and for the way in which the jaunty rhythms of the 'Spanish Caprice' (the film's proper title – changed to try and lure the public) accompany the differing moods and pace of the three main characters. The veils, flowers, combs and nets in which Dietrich is framed throughout the action reach a moment of supreme beauty in the scene that she herself chooses to represent the film: Conchita is surprised by her middle-aged lover while entertaining another man in her rooms; she moves from the back of the room through several dark net curtains, then stands with her hands raised, holding back the drapes, framed by tousled hair, black sequins and one of the most perfect examples of the 'Sternberg effect' – her face transformed into a sculptural essay in light and shade. When dialogue resumes and she begins to rant and rave at Lionel Atwill, the contrast between the beauty of her apparition and the violence of their exchange merely adds to the viewers' exhilaration.

In later years Dietrich was always at pains to make it clear that it was von Sternberg who left her, not the other way round. The four films that followed the ending of their collaboration all attempted to create a 'new' Dietrich in place of the von Sternberg formula, while still clinging to the lighting, costumes and romantic settings that had characterized the von Sternberg-Dietrich films. Each has its pleasures: *Desire* marks Dietrich's reunion with Gary Cooper; and *The Garden of Allah*, despite its unlikely settings and plot, deserves mention for the beauty of early Technicolor and for Dietrich's tenderness with Charles Boyer, especially in their final farewell scene. Then came that British public schoolboy's fantasy on the subject of the Russian Revolution, *Knight without Armour*. It was exquisitely photographed by Harry Stradling, especially the long, silent sequence in which the young countess is shown awakening to an empty house, where the only sounds are the different tones of bells and buzzers as she impotently attempts to summon help. Dietrich, dressed in white and standing in the sunlight, is then seen from above facing the revolutionary mob, which is approaching in the shadows; the camera moves in to a close shot as she demands, 'What are you waiting for?'

After this British film, Dietrich returned to Hollywood and Paramount for a film that has been largely misunderstood and unjustly criticized, Ernst Lubitsch's *Angel*. It is a slow, sad variation on the eternal triangle, in which Dietrich is partnered perfectly by Herbert Marshall as her husband, and less probably by Melvyn Douglas as her lover. With its brooding pre-war mood of menace, it has something in common with those films made in France around the same time, in which, although it is not mentioned, every action and character seems to be overwhelmed by the coming war. Although Lubitsch is most famous as a director of light comedies, this melancholy film, in which Dietrich is glacially beautiful throughout ('raising and lowering at intervals artificial eyelashes you could hang a hat on', in Theodore Huff's cruel but memorable phrase), is today one of her most perfect and enjoyable appearances as the total Dietrich character. Lubitsch was shortly afterwards to direct Garbo in *Ninotchka*. A characteristic both actresses had in common was an ability, in George Cukor's words, to 'create eroticism. It's the uncensored thought the actor flashes to the audience . . . she could let them know she was thinking things, and thinking them uncensored.' Uncensored or not, *Angel* was not a success, and on 4 May 1938 a red-bordered advertisement appeared in the *Hollywood Reporter* – placed by the Independent Theatre Owner's Association of New York – in which several famous Hollywood stars were labelled 'Box-Office Poison'. Prominent among the names was that of Marlene Dietrich.

Beaton: The First Session

Cecil Beaton considered that away from the camera Dietrich was 'more exotic, more extraordinary'. Her first portrait session with Beaton took place in Salzburg in 1935: no lights were available, it was pouring with rain and Dietrich had a head cold. Nevertheless, she got out of bed and agreed to pose lying on the floor, with a white table-cloth as a lighting prop. Without make-up, and with none of the spotlights that created the famous lighting effect of shadows under the nose and around the cheek-bones, Beaton noticed that 'most striking of her features is her whiteness, which would put the moon or a white rabbit to shame, even though, as she explains, she uses a powder darker than the colour of her skin'. Beaton later wrote that he was reminded, at least by the results of this session, of certain portraits of the great Italian actress, Eleonora Duse.

In Vogue

Having established a definite rapport with her, Beaton took many photographs of Dietrich in Hollywood and in New York. He recalled that he wanted to prove she could be photographed in many different sorts of lighting, not just using the 'Sternberg effect'; however, the results of the first Hollywood session displeased her sufficiently for her to tear up the contact sheets. These photographs were taken at the Waldorf in New York, where Beaton said his rooms looked as if a tornado had swept through them after he had experimented with dozens of effects. 'I know of no other actress who is so enthusiastic in taking up suggestions about new make-ups and general appearance,' wrote Beaton. Fifty years later Dietrich still named him as one of her five favourite photographers (the others were Avedon, Steichen, Snowdon and Milton Greene). Unlike Garbo, surmised Beaton, Dietrich was 'entirely interested in the effect she makes on her limitless public'.

FUR ENOUGH

In the 1930s the transatlantic voyage was as much a feature of a Hollywood personality's way of life as the TV chat-show or phone-in is today. Dietrich's acceptance of her part in the publicity machine that became an integral part of her career resulted in largely friendly relations with press photographers, none of whom was going to be able to achieve the same lighting effects that she might have expected from the likes of Beaton or Horst. Because of this, the photographs taken on board the *Berengaria*, *en route* to New York with her husband, are remarkable, showing the extent to which she had studied her image so that in public it corresponded to her latest screen roles. The python-skin handbag with polished art-deco handle, the cluster of gold beads at her neck and the fur coat cut in swaggering trench-coat style are all set off by the elaborately stitched gloves. The teddy-bear type coat worn by the photographer on the right seems to balance the star's outfit perfectly.

THE MISSING LYNX

The Paramount publicity department usefully identified the colour scheme of this 1936 outfit, *right*: pale brown wool skirt ('the length is new, note the pleats in front'), dark brown blouse with detachable 'Ascot' scarf, brown hat with a single goose quill and beige cape. The extravagant swathe of red fox, which kept Douglas Fairbanks Jr at a respectful distance at a film première in the same season, *above*, makes Constance Collier's modest little cape, black velvet gown and pearls look almost dowdy. Miss Collier had been instrumental in introducing Fairbanks Sr to Chaplin, thus helping to launch what was to become United Artists. A veteran of Hollywood, Broadway and the West End, Collier complained of the movies, 'When you had finished your day's work you were generally too tired to go to Los Angeles, so you would go home, have a bath, change your clothes and meet the same people over and over again. You either had to love them or hate them; there was nothing else possible.' As for Douglas Fairbanks Jr, Dietrich once declared that he had the knack of picking up and digesting only the best parts of what he encountered on his travels. Like Dietrich, he retained an enduring and glamorous public persona for over sixty years.

WARM FOR JUNE

Jean Cocteau once wrote that when Dietrich wore 'furs and plumes' she did so 'as the birds and animals wear them, as though they belong to your body'. Von Sternberg had exploited this characteristic to the full in his films, and both costume designers and photographers were always on the alert to use the softness of fur to offset the hardness of Dietrich's make-up, which

resembled a Chinese mask in some of her films. The furs in *Blonde Venus*, *below*, and *Desire*, *opposite*, both achieve this effect. For some reason Dietrich, photographed in London in June 1936, *right*, seems to be dressed for winter in a mink cape and long velvet gauntlets, while her companions' garb is comparatively summery. The young man asking for an autograph on the left seems undecided about whether to pose for the camera or attend to the object of his idolatry.

TRAVIS BANTON

All Dietrich's films at Paramount were costumed by Travis Banton. He, together with von Sternberg, was responsible for the black feathers of *Shanghai Express*, the gorilla suit of *Blonde Venus*, the fur-lined cloaks of *Scarlet Express* and the clinging gowns and cartwheel hats of *The Devil is a Woman*. Towards the end of the 1930s, after Dietrich's break with von Sternberg and at the end of that whole period of European-oriented Hollywood movies, Banton designed striking variations on the lounge-pyjama for her. These suited the casual sexiness of Dietrich's role in *Desire*, *right*, and departed from the more formalized aspects of the costumes she had worn in von Sternberg's melodramas. Dietrich acknowledged Banton's contribution to the creation of her screen image, especially the way he helped her to achieve the effect von Sternberg intended. A Texan who had been apprenticed to the then-famous New York dressmaker Frances, Banton came to Hollywood in 1924 and designed the costumes for dozens of films for Paramount, and later for Fox and Universal. The outfit, *opposite*, was designed to be worn at home.

P 1167-

ALMOST A GENTLEMAN

Dietrich's ability to carry off wearing masculine garb, while still retaining her femininity, and hint at a flavour of androgyny was accentuated by Josef von Sternberg in all but their final film, *The Devil is a Woman*. She wears a top hat in *Blue Angel*, *Morocco* and *Blonde Venus*; in *Shanghai Express* she dons a military coat and a peaked cap; in *Scarlet Empress* she rides to her victory in a white cossack uniform, and in *Dishonored* she is dressed either as a helmeted demigod, an aviator, or in mannish collar and tie. The tweed suit or belted trench-coats, worn with slanted berets, together with the summery two-piece efforts with a Naval cap are all reflected over thirty years later in some of Dietrich's outfits on her extended world tours. Dietrich complained that the setting of the trend for women to wear men's clothes was attributed to her incorrectly. It is true that actresses as far back in time as Nell Gwyn had been donning trousers in an effort to seem liberated or just to show off their ankles, but what Dietrich made fashionable was the use of the mannish cut for women. As for tweed suits, she eventually decided that only Englishmen should wear them – no one else could look elegant in heavy brown-soled shoes. It has to be remembered when looking at the trousers, that until the end of the 1930s the very notion of a respectable woman wearing trousers was frowned upon in conventional households.

LINE PERFECT

When Dietrich was rehearsing
her lines for Rouben
Mamoulian's *Song of Songs*,
right, in 1933, her trousers
were already notorious. 'Sorry,'
said the publicity department,
'Dietrich does not wear them in
the picture.' The pose and style
are in vivid contrast to the role
she plays in the film, which is
memorable not only for the
scene in which she
accompanies herself at the
piano and sings Schubert's
'Heidenroslein', but also for the
nude statue, for which she is
said to have posed. Even then
Dietrich was wary of her
'legendary image', so the fate
that befell the statue, *opposite*,
was perhaps satisfying.

ARTWORK

Rouben Mamoulian, seated, and Brian Aherne, in white tie, watch the action, while Dietrich destroys her own image. She had not wished to make this film adaptation of Edward Sheldon's play, adapted in its turn from the novel by Hermann Sudermann. It was the beginning of the break with von Sternberg, and perhaps her amnesia about the whole affair led to the later, rather curious conflict of facts surrounding the song from the cabaret scene. In the black dress she is wearing here, she sings Holländer's 'Johnny' in English. At every concert in the 1950s, 1960s and 1970s she sang this song in German and would always announce that she was doing so 'because no English words were ever written for it'. It was on the set of *Song of Songs* that she once crept up to the microphone and whispered, 'Joe, where are you?'

CHASTE TASTE

If Dietrich was wary of her public image and came to detest the 'legend', she was equally jealous of guarding the privacy of her own home and family. This is one of the few portraits of her taken 'at home', showing what the studio publicity department described coyly as her 'chaste taste'. Cecil Beaton reported that her house was dominated by the smell of coffee and the sweet marzipan cakes that Dietrich and her daughter cooked up in the kitchen, mixed with 'the whiff of greasepaint'. As in all her other residences, the piano dominated the room. Had she not studied the violin, Dietrich wrote, she might have considered the piano as her instrument. Her musical ability becomes the somewhat far-fetched theme of von Sternberg's *Dishonored*, in which she uses musical notation as a form of secret writing. As for looking after the house, Dietrich's mania for doing the housework – always travelling with cans of cleaning fluid – was a favourite topic with interviewers. Housework, she maintained, was the best form of occupational therapy. 'Miss Dietrich lives very quietly,' insisted the studio copywriters, 'with her daughter and a minimum of servants.' The mixture of art-deco mirror effects, Chinese wallpaper, bamboo frames and black lacquer tables is a startling contrast to the interior of the Siebers' apartment in Berlin seven years earlier. The heavy bookcases filled with leather-bound tomes have given way to the zebra-skin print day bed with shiny black pillows; the portrait study by Marie Laurencin (perhaps not of Dietrich herself) is given pride of place in the bedroom.

3

Although the reasons behind the 'Box-Office Poison' tag may have been politically motivated – as Kenneth Anger suggests with scurrilous glee in his notorious *Hollywood Babylon* – the effect was predictable: Dietrich's contract with Paramount was not renewed and it did not seem likely that more film offers would come from the USA or England. In 1938 the Siebers spent most of their time in France, although Dietrich now acknowledges that she was living with Erich Maria Remarque, author of *All Quiet on Western Front*; Maria was at school in Switzerland and it was announced that Dietrich would film in France with Raimu, the character actor famous for his roles in Marcel Pagnol's films *Marius* and *La Femme du Boulanger*.

Just before war broke out, Dietrich received an offer from Joe Pasternak, the head of production at Universal Studios: would she come back to Hollywood and play a role in comic western? The film, *Destry Rides Again*, overturns the usual formula by having for its hero a deputy-sheriff (played by James Stewart) who doesn't carry a gun and who is all for non-violent solutions. The local gangland boss runs a saloon where the crooked poker games are arranged with the connivance of his girlfriend, the hardbitten, brawling singer Frenchy; this was the role he wanted Dietrich to play. As von Sternberg was staying in France with her, Dietrich asked his advice; he said she should go.

Pasternak met her at the station in Los Angeles and immediately started coaching her for the part. 'I took out a pouch of tobacco and some cigarette papers,' he wrote, 'blew at one until I had a single paper. Then with one hand, using my teeth to open the neck of the pouch, I dropped tobacco on the paper, wet the length of it, closed the pouch and held out the makings to her. "What are you doing?" she asked. "Showing you the first thing I want you to learn. I want you to be able to make a smoke for yourself with one hand." '

As Frenchy, Dietrich engages in a rolling-on-the-floor, hair-pulling, eye-scratching fight with Una Merkel, who plays a jealous wife whose husband loses his trousers in a poker game; Frenchy is then doused with a pail of water by Deputy-Sheriff Destry and proceeds to attempt to murder him with a chair leg. Friedrich Holländer wrote two of his best numbers for her: 'You've Got That Look' and 'The Boys in the Backroom'.

Dietrich gives a new variant on her volte-face technique for the very last moment of the film. As brassy and hard as can be, her affection for Tom Destry leads Frenchy to place her body in the way of the assassin's bullet in the climactic fight. As she dies in his arms she whispers, 'Aren't you going to kiss me goodbye?', wipes the lipstick off her mouth, kisses him and dies. This tear-jerking scene appealed to the new sense of morality that was beginning to invade movies. In her earlier roles the Dietrich character might get her man and even keep him, no matter how bad she appeared to be on the surface; now she had to sacrifice him, even at the cost of her life. *Destry* was a big success; it re-established Dietrich in Hollywood and allowed her to pay off the taxman and to help a number of friends – in particular Erich Maria Remarque – in their efforts to live in the comparative safety of the USA.

Dietrich's following film, *Seven Sinners*, never enjoyed the fame of *Destry*, but is in many ways much more enjoyable. It is a subtle spoof on the theme of the loose woman who gets mixed up with a younger, respectable man – in this case John Wayne – and eventually lets him go off with the eligible girl-next-door type (played with good humour by Anna Lee). In the most famous sequence Dietrich, dressed in a white Naval officer's uniform, sings 'The Man's in the Navy' and then flirts with Wayne, who is identically dressed. She sends him back to the Navy and in the closing scene settles for a shipboard affair with a seedy, semi-alcoholic doctor.

Seven Sinners, and most of the other films Dietrich made over the next two years (*Manpower*, *Pittsburgh*, *The Spoilers*), are all variants on the buddy-movie in which Dietrich plays the more or less wicked woman with whom the tough guys get temporarily involved. The exception is René Clair's *The Flame of New Orleans*, a film that could have been much more effective with stronger male leads. It has Dietrich in a dual role as an adventuress posing as a countess who is then forced into pretending to be her own sister. She haunts a dockside dive and makes off on her wedding day with the ship's captain who has found her out. It is as light as any comedy Clair made, but the 'bad sister' character does not get enough time on screen and Dietrich's little-girl-innocent act becomes tiresome.

Dietrich was bored by most of these parts, although she says of Pasternak, 'He was not a director but a producer, I don't know where he is now but I loved him very much . . . I can't tell why I accepted a role. It was either that Wharft got me on the phone and said, "Would you do the film?" and I said yes or no, whatever. I did not really read every script carefully . . . If you don't take your career as unseriously as I have taken mine you would always go for good directors. So what the hell. It's another film. You see I always had a distance. I never fell for Hollywood.' Pasternak said that working with Dietrich, even though he was 'just the window – that's all the producer ever is', was an unforgettable experience. He found her a 'most self-conscious' woman, who knew every inch of her art and was aware at every moment of what she should be doing. If this never gave an impression of effortlessness, he concluded that 'she is not vain. I am not surprised when I read that the woman who has attended her in the powder room of a famous New York night-club reports that in twenty years she has never seen Miss Dietrich stop or make up at the mirror. Marlene is studied where it counts.'

After the three Pasternak films at Universal, Dietrich went over to Warner Brothers for *Manpower*, a film notable for the hitherto unlikely sight of Dietrich baking biscuits in a modern kitchen, and also for the hospital scenes, in which she and some of the patients smoke cigarettes enthusiastically in the ward. The greatest Warner Brothers leading lady of the 1940s was of course Bette Davis. Like Dietrich, Davis had done spates of selling war bonds in the first months of 1942, and when she returned to Hollywood she and John Garfield founded the Hollywood Canteen for servicemen. 'The whole idea of the canteen was to give the men fun, relaxation and the chance to meet personally and be served by the stars of Hollywood and not be charged one cent,' wrote Davis. 'Some, like Dietrich, not only contributed glamour out front but backbreaking labour in the kitchen.'

Dietrich had long been a member of something called the 'Hollywood committee' (organized by Ernst Lubitsch and Billy Wilder among others) which had contributed funds before the war to help refugees from Germany travel to the USA. After the entry of America into the European war, Dietrich says she started to plan her exit from Hollywood in order to go with the American forces to Europe. Her final films were a wartime revue, *Follow the Boys* – in which she appears in a conjuring act with Orson

Welles – and her first and only appearance with MGM, her legs painted gold, as the harem favourite Jamilla in *Kismet*, a film she ironically refers to in her autobiography as 'this masterpiece'.

Dietrich had taken American citizenship, but both Rudolf Sieber and Erich Maria Remarque were classified as 'enemy aliens' and were thus rendered unable to apply for jobs. In order to support them, Dietrich continued to work until she was finally called up and taken to be trained as a member of the armed forces. She was then sent to areas behind enemy lines, first of all to North Africa, then Italy and finally the countries of central Europe where the war continued.

Dietrich had already made a number of recordings in German of popular American songs, which were broadcast as part of the Americans' wartime propaganda; Lotte Lenya did the same. While she was in New York in 1943, Dietrich had a number of meetings and even signed a contract to appear as Venus in a musical comedy by Kurt Weill to be called *One Touch of Venus*. In her interviews in the 1960s (when the legendary aspect of the Berlin nightlife of the 1920s had already replaced any realism) Dietrich used to insist that, despite the roles she had played, she had had 'nothing' to do with the music-theatre world of Weill and Brecht. Nevertheless, she knew Weill well enough to have requested some songs from him for possible recordings, and he had written two for her in 1934. Nothing had come of this, but she had been sufficiently interested to consider playing Venus, and had visited the Metropolitan Museum to study different paintings and sculptures. (Anstey's novel, on which the show was to be based, concerns a statue that is brought to life.) However, when Bella Spewack and Ogden Nash submitted their dialogue and lyrics Dietrich rejected them. According to Weill's biographer, Ronald Sanders, 'She called it "too sexy and profane", and protested that, as the mother of a nineteen-year-old daughter, she could no longer display herself on a stage the way she once did.' Still, she had gone as far as to try out her voice on the stage of the 46th Street Theatre, and she had had no difficulty in putting a number across.

Pasternak, William Diertele (who directed *Kismet*), Weill, Lenya and Clair were all refugees from the war in Europe. So was Jean Gabin, with whom Dietrich, in the

1940s, began a long and close friendship in Hollywood. Gabin eventually returned to Europe as a member of the Free French forces, by which time Dietrich was a Captain in the American Army. As an entertainer during the years 1943–46, Dietrich became a camp-follower, a real-life version of the roles she had played so convincingly in von Sternberg's abstractions, *Morocco* and *Dishonored* (although she always reminds us, 'don't confuse the actor with the task'.) The experience of playing to these huge audiences of enlisted men brought Dietrich back into contact with an audience, and the most difficult one imaginable. She later said that if you can gain the attention of men who know that in a few hours they may be killed or maimed, then you can do anything. Her friend Noël Coward also asserted that after these troop concerts anything else was 'gravy'.

It was in North Africa that British troops had first been able to pick up the German forces' radio stations and had learned the marching song 'Lili Marlene'. Because of its gloomily romantic theme – the soldier who waits for the prostitute under the lamp – it had been banned by the German authorities as an insult to German womanhood and a poor influence on the morale of the men. However, the radio stations kept on playing it, announcing another record and then putting on Lale Andersen's original record 'by mistake'. It was taken up in France, where Suzy Solidor, the deep-voiced blonde *chanteuse* who ran her own cabaret ('La Vie Parisienne'), recorded it, as did the Italian opera star Gianna Pederzini. 'Because of the name it's connected with me all over the world,' Dietrich has said. 'I know Fassbinder made a film about it – ridiculous film – but in English-speaking countries the song is connected with me.'

Dietrich's wartime act, when she had the benefit of a theatre or hall to play in (often she had to travel in a jeep with her accompanist and put over her numbers from the back of a truck or in a shed), usually began with a comedian coming on to the stage and announcing to the expectant audience that Dietrich wasn't going to be there after all, as she had been invited out to dinner with a General. Amidst the groans of disappointment a voice from the back would call out, 'I'm here, I'm here,' and Dietrich would run down the gangway in her uniform, carrying a case. She would then produce a pair of evening shoes and a dress, and after making as if to start changing on stage, would be led off decorously into the wings, to the whistles of encouragement from the men. 'No Love, No Nothing', 'Lazy Afternoon', 'Annie Doesn't Live Here Any More' and 'The Boys in the Backroom' were staples of her repertory, as was the song that would eventually become ubiquitous, 'Lili Marlene'. She also revived her musical saw, which for years had been a feature of her party-turn in Hollywood.

When Dietrich departed for 'Destination Unknown', her 55 lb baggage allowance, according to a *Vogue* report, comprised the following: two long, sequined gowns (so heavily encrusted with beads that no crease would show); a strapless brocade dress; transparent Vinylite slippers; grey flannel men's trousers; silk-lined cashmere jumper by Mainbocher; tropical uniforms; and lingerie. She also carried three months' supply of cosmetics, labelled in huge nail-polish letters (for dressing by torchlight), and a supply of special soap for her hair that she had had specially made, and which would lather in practically no water.

Danny Thomas, a comedian and compère, was instrumental in teaching Dietrich how to manipulate the audience, time her laughs and deal with hecklers. During her time with the forces, the whole way in which she presented herself as a performer underwent a change. This could be seen not only in the self-deprecating humour with which she quietly derided her glamorous image – something that she has retained until today, as in her famous dismissal of much of her glamour and mystery as 'kitsch' or 'quatsch' – but in her very delivery of the songs. Whereas on the records made in Los Angeles in the early 1940s we can hear the studied heavy-breathing, the effortful and deliberate 'sexiness' associated with the vamp, once she began to enact her real-life experiences as a *vivandière* on record a merrier and simpler way of putting over a song can be heard (for example, in her selections of old hits like 'Je Sais que Vous Êtes Jolie', 'Das Alte Lied' or 'Ich Weiss Nicht zu Wem Ich Gehöre').

Dietrich contracted pneumonia in Italy in 1944, and in the Ardennes her hands froze. In May 1944, when she was out on an assignment with Jean-Pierre Aumont (the French matinée idol and star of dozens of films from *Lac aux Dames* to Truffaut's *La Nuit Américaine*), they found themselves lost in No Man's Land during the assault on Cassino. In his diary, Aumont described her: 'In her khaki uniform, her mop of golden hair stuck under a cap, she went from camp to camp, from hospital to hospital, singing for the American soldiers. I asked her to come and sing for us. She jumped into my jeep. Night fell. I lost the way . . . To be taken prisoner wasn't a particularly agreeable prospect for me, but to responsible for Marlene's capture . . . Without doubt she would have been shot . . . But Marlene Dietrich, despite what the "legend" would have one believe, is a courageous and tough woman. No tears. No panic. When she took the decision to go and sing behind the lines, she knew what the risks were. She took them with no regrets, with a swagger, without boasting. By driving around we managed to get back behind the lines . . .' There were other occasions when Dietrich found herself in a dangerous position, often with battalions that were surrounded. When she was decorated by the Americans and the French it was not just for services rendered, but also for bravery.

The decision to join the Army was a brave one, and it must have been difficult to make, suggested Maximlian Schell in their 1984 interview. No, asserted Dietrich, there was nothing brave about it. Everyone wanted to end the war, to stop the advance of Hitler. What decision was there? 'We knew about the concentration camps and we knew they were killing women and children and we wanted it to stop.' And as a German? Her reply has become part of the Dietrich legend: 'I'm a German, and I understand the Germans. They all want a leader. We all do, that's what Germans are like. They wanted their Führer. And they got him.' Even in the 1970s she was still receiving letters asking her why she had left Germany. She returned them, scrawling across the bottom 'Well known'.

In 1944 Dietrich was reunited with Jean Gabin. Since she has so often stated that her private life was entirely separate from her life as a performer, it is not possible to take entirely seriously the statements she has made about those with whom she became involved outside the studio. However, since Dietrich on a number of occasions chose to single out Gabin – paying him the compliment of citing him as her ideal of manhood – there is no reason to believe that she was fooling. They first met in Hollywood when he was filming there after the fall of France in 1940. Along with Jean Renoir, and even René Clair ('not the friendliest of people'), he was a frequent guest at Dietrich's house and she claimed that she taught him to speak English correctly for his first US film. But his real desire was to return to Europe and join the Free French Army, and he eventually did so. After the war they were both in Paris, and there was talk of their appearing together in the Carné-Prévert film, *Les Portes de la Nuit*, but in the end they pulled out. Both were without work, and they had to endure interviews with people who wondered at their long absence from the screen. Eventually they made a film together, *Martin Roumagnac*. This is a gloomy melodrama set in a provincial French town, and it has all the uncertainty of a film made in a country attempting to recover from the trauma of occupation and war, but at the same time retreating behind a smoke-screen of escapist nostalgia. Dietrich's one-time partner from the days of *Es Liegt in der Luft*, Margo Lion, had a small part in the film. It is difficult to imagine the postwar Dietrich finding a slot in the new European cinema that eventually emerged from the ruins. She was forced to return to the USA and Gabin stayed in France.

In 1963 Dietrich found herself sitting beside Robert Kennedy at a party given by William Walton. According to Arthur Schlesinger, Bobby 'with his innocent audacity' asked Dietrich who had been the most attractive man she had ever known, to which she answered immediately, 'Jean Gabin.' Their years together, she said, had been the happiest of her life. Schlesinger continues, 'Bobby asked why she had left him. She said, "Because he wanted to marry me." When Bobby expressed surprise, she said, "I hate marriage. It is an immoral institution. I told him that if I stayed with him it was because I was in love with him, and that was all that mattered." Bobby asked whether she still saw him. She said, "No, he won't see me any more. He has married, and has grown terribly fat, and thinks he is no longer attractive, and does not want me to see him."' Robert Kennedy then asked Marlene Dietrich if she thought that Gabin still loved her. She replied, 'Of course.'

SUMMER OF '39

American movie distributors labelled Dietrich one of those stars who were 'Box-Office Poison'. As a result, Dietrich spent most of the year preceding the outbreak of war in September 1939 in France. There were plans – never realized – for her to make a film with Raimu, and she was photographed hobnobbing with stars of the Paris stage, including Cecile Sorel, *below*, and Mistinguett. Rudolf Sieber was working in France, as was Erich Maria Remarque *overleaf*. Dietrich's friendship with Remarque was one of the closest of her life. When war came, she helped him to move to the United States.

All Quiet on the L.A. Front

In Hollywood in 1940, Dietrich's career was baled out by Joe Pasternak at Universal Studios, who cast her as the brawling saloon hostess, Frenchy, in *Destry Rides Again*. In this, and in her two subsequent comedies made for Universal, Dietrich effectively sends up her glamorous image without detracting from her on-screen beauty. *Seven Sinners*, *right* with Willie Fung and *overleaf*, is even more enjoyable than *Destry*, and remains one of her best films. It is a comedy of sexual manners, underscored with the theme of coming to terms with age. Bijou, the *chanteuse*, cruises around the South Seas and offsets her extravagantly vulgar costumes - veils and feathers and rhinestones in broad sunlight – by surrounding herself with young Naval officers. As in most of Dietrich's films, she makes play with a cigarette to occupy her hands.

SHOULDER PADS

Dietrich discusses *The Flame of New Orleans* with its director, René Clair, on the Universal Studios lot. She is wearing a 1940s outfit with wide shoulders and patch pockets. The contemporary fashions were skilfully reflected in the film's period costumes, designed by René Hubert.

CIGARETT-IQUETTE

The open box of cigarettes on the mirror-topped table belongs to an era when entertaining involved always having cigarettes, usually several types, available for guests. Dietrich developed a real flourish with cigarettes – holder or no holder – and this added to her allure, even when her arm was in a sling; she was even stopped for an autograph by a French customs official.

Don't Smoke in Bed

Cigarettes were an essential feature of Dietrich's screen persona, and featured in the plot devices of so many of her films that it is a surprise to find photographs of her not holding a cigarette. In *Dishonored* a message is secreted in the hollow tube of an Imperial Russian cigarette; in *The Devil is a Woman* Concha is first seen working in a cigarette factory; and in her own favourite role, as the fortune-telling Madame in *Touch of Evil*, a novel twist is added by the character's smoking a long cheroot. Between her long fingers, the nails varnished a shiny red, the presence of a dog-end was deemed not to detract from the high glamour of off-screen portraits in the 1930s, *previous spread*. Wherever she went, Dietrich was seen smoking: sitting beside Jean Gabin at the wheel, with Erich Maria Remarque in a restaurant, with Charles Chaplin in the corridor of the Comédie Française, duelling with young reporters in London, and smoking instead of eating at the 'Diadem Ball' in Paris. In the 1960s Dietrich had a bet with Noël Coward and gave up smoking. At about the same time she took to singing Peggy Lee's old standard, 'Don't Smoke in Bed', but she continued to encourage other people to defy the anti-smokers.

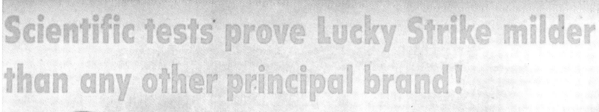

STUDIO
SESSION

This study, taken in 1942,
shows what the lighting director
within Dietrich could achieve:
the sinister and the soulful
combined in the same
enigmatic expression.

Marching Song

Dietrich had been a stalwart of the Hollywood canteen, contributing glamour out front and back-breaking labour in the kitchens. Here she is performing at the London branch of the stage-door canteen, in September 1944. It is difficult not to believe, from the look of uninhibited enthusiasm on her face, her later assertion that she had left Hollywood behind without a twinge of regret. Both she and her daughter, Maria, entertained troops in the USA before embarking for Europe.

OH CAPTAIN, MY CAPTAIN

In North Africa Dietrich was seen signing autographs, getting her shoes cleaned and lending her particular brand of humour to the post-invasion morale. Twenty years later she appeared at the El Alamein Reunion in London. What had been important, she maintained, as well as the victory was 'the sharing. Then it was "Share my food, my water, my danger." Nowadays you've got to hang on to what you've got or it's snatched from you. Sharing was a positive good we could practise now. But surely no human being in the world likes war . . . Tonight I sing for the ones who live and who want to live.'

JEEPS AND GENERALS

Hemingway was to write, 'She is as lovely looking in the morning in a GI shirt, pants and combat boots as she is at night or on the screen.' Dietrich's wartime service wound up in France, where she officially purchased the jeep, *La Grande*, in which she had been touring. She returned later for the Liberation of Paris anniversary ceremony in 1951, and much later for a gala at the Palais de Chaillot, where she encountered her hero, President de Gaulle. She said that in her eyes he could do no wrong; his code of conduct was the personification of what she believed in. At this historic confrontation, Maria Schell, Giulietta Masina and Danielle Darrieux look on.

QUAND L'AMOUR MEURT

A farewell that was to prove final. As Dietrich left France in August 1946, to return to Hollywood, Jean Gabin carried her bags to the aircraft. Their longtime friendship had resulted in the less than successful *Martin Roumagnac*, *below* and *overleaf*, in which Dietrich was cast, improbably and unwisely, as a Frenchwoman with an Australian accent.

A new era, but the same old routine. On board the *Queen Elizabeth* in 1947, Dietrich's buttons are emblazoned with 'M' and she is wearing huge-tongued shoes. She told reporters that she was trying to put on some weight to 'improve the curves a little'.

4

HOLLYWOOD -

LAS VEGAS

Kenneth Tynan wrote an appreciation of Dietrich in the early 1950s. 'She has three Ds, in the Hollywood sense of the phrase, but should the third dimension break down, she will always be able (as they say of airliners) to limp home on the other two.' This somewhat backhanded compliment sums up how perilous Dietrich's status was in the American cinema immediately after World War II. To speak of her limping home would have seemed incongruous, even outrageous, before 1941. However, in the early Cold War period of the late 1940s – marked by the paranoic atmosphere of McCarthyism – Dietrich's exotic and totally European brand of sophisticated humour began to prove difficult to market to the new television public, or to present as an alternative to the rising group of youth-dominated idols. Dietrich's great contemporaries, Garbo and Mae West, had both quit the studios, and her successors, Rita Hayworth and Ingrid Bergman, were already long established. Although Dietrich and her peers had been no older than Grace Kelly, Marilyn Monroe or James Dean when their careers became successful, the earlier stars had always seemed to be much more mature and worldly figures on the screen.

It was left to a British studio and a director (Hitchcock with *Stage Fright*) to experiment with the chemistry of teaming Dietrich with a noticeably younger leading man – thereby capturing the mood of *Rosenkavalier* dalliance that she could hint at so well. This was reminiscent of those roles of the 1930s, when her brilliant *hauteur* on the screen rendered the likes of Boyer and Donat almost infantile. Meanwhile, in Hollywood in 1947, she returned to Paramount after a ten-year absence, to play a central European gypsy in Mitchell Leisen's *Golden Earrings*. Her fee was about half what she would have been paid before the war, Dietrich asserts, but when in need 'you're ready to do anything'.

The role of Lydia in *Golden Earrings* is such a departure from Dietrich's accepted image that it is a shame the comic-book escape/adventure plot should be quite as absurd as it is. Wearing a black wig, draped in shawls, scarves and jewellery, her body painted a dark colour and her eyebrows thickened to an extraordinary degree, Dietrich plays a fish-stew boiling, fortune-telling gypsy who hides an escaped English spy in her caravan and outwits several parties of belligerent but dimwited stormtroopers in the weeks leading up to the outbreak of war in 1939. The part gave her an opportunity to play the cymbalo, drive horses and mutter endearments in German to the charming but miscast Ray Milland, whose eyes take on a wicked glow when he speaks of his pierced ears (Dietrich is shown performing this feat, too, with an apparently unsterilized needle). The plight of the gypsies in Europe, their persecution by the Nazis and the incongruity of their presence when war is declared in the climactic scene, is touched on only once, when Lydia mutters gloomily, 'One day, in this accursed land, they will kill all of us.' Her cohorts are dressed as if for a Johann Strauss operetta, their nineteenth-century costumes romantically contrasted with the jackbooted villains.

This film would have been sufficient to put paid to anyone else's career, yet Dietrich emerged from it apparently unscathed and immediately went on to star in another film that was set in war-torn Germany. *A Foreign Affair* is a black comedy set in Berlin during the Allied occupation; Dietrich gives one of the finest performances of her career, and Billy Wilder's direction has all the speed and irony for which he is famous. (It is worth noting that Wilder provided the three greatest glamour stars of Hollywood with their most completely enjoyable movies; for Garbo, *Ninotchka* – for which Wilder wrote the script; for Dietrich, *A Foreign Affair*; and for Marilyn Monroe, *Some Like It Hot*.)

At first Dietrich had to be persuaded to play Erika, the girlfriend of a Nazi official. It is her least sympathetic role: Erika knows no pity or compassion, and manipulates her 'Johnny' shamelessly (each role in which she has to pronounce this name offers her an echo of her once-famous hit record). A glimmer of postwar realism creeps in when we first glimpse Erika in her bathrobe, her mouth full of toothpaste. But the three set-piece night-club scenes, in which Dietrich – with Holländer himself at the piano – sings 'Black Market', 'Illusions' and 'The Ruins of Berlin', are (together with *The Blue Angel* and *Destry*) the epitome of everything for which Dietrich the screen *chanteuse* is renowned. (Ten years later, Wilder was to provide Dietrich with another role as a survivor of the war in Germany, this time in the flash-back sequence at the beginning of *Witness for the Prosecution*.) After *A Foreign Affair* this enjoyable interlude seemed to have been exhausted, and Dietrich returned to Europe to appear in Alfred

Hitchcock's *Stage Fright*. This film gave her another opportunity to demonstrate the technique of her volte-face: in her role as the accomplice of her husband's murderer, she fends off police and reporters with a display of backstage temperament, but when unmasked by the wily Jane Wyman character she reveals her real self with a line about once having had a dog as a pet, but 'he bit me. So I had him shot.' This scene was filmed entirely from above, and contains one of the very greatest close-ups of Dietrich who, at the age of fifty, still achieved a remarkable smoothness in her public demeanour. This is accentuated by the wardrobe, which was designed by Christian Dior for this movie and for the one she made shortly afterwards, *No Highway*.

After her daughter Maria gave birth to a son in 1946, Dietrich was dubbed by the American press 'the world's most glamorous grandmother'; she lived up to this new, somewhat incongruous aspect of her image by dressing with the delightful formality that Dior provided with his 'New Look'. (This term was invented by the American media – Dior himself never used it for his collections.) Dietrich had been to his first collection in 1947: 'I went to Dior when he first started,' she told Cynthia Kee in 1960. 'There hasn't been any fashion since that. There is fashion in magazines, but where are these dresses we see in them? I never see them being worn. But since Dior made his great revolution, what change has there been? Waists here, waists there, flat – what does it mean?' Dior's long, full skirts, tightly-waisted jackets, formal high-heeled shoes, and hats with floating veils all had a pre-World War I romanticism, but also a certain severity which suited Dietrich in her late forties. Among her own outfits was a back-buttoning dress, a favourite Dior touch ('A haberdasher's dream come true,' said *Vogue*), and two-piece suits that were typical of Dior's 'vertical' and 'oblique' lines of 1950. Describing these collections, Brigid Keenan noted that 'many of the garments were made entirely in tucked or pleated cloths', and it is one of these dresses that is a key element in the plot of *Stage Fright*. The film begins with a red-herring device in which Richard Todd tells a lie that is enacted on the screen – a scene in which Dietrich is wearing a bloodstained dress. This elaborate plot device confused many people and has led to the film's being generally underrated in Hitchcock's *oeuvre*. In his monumental study of Alfred Hitchcock's films, the French critic Bruno Villien makes an analogy between Dietrich's rapport on screen with Richard Todd, and Colette's Chéri and Léa.

For the musical comedy sequence in *Stage Fright*, Cole Porter rewrote a song that had been lying dormant in his archive since 1927. The number was called 'The Laziest Gal in Town'; Dietrich sings it swooningly, draping herself romantically on a series of *chaises-longues*. (When she incorporated it into her song repertory later, it was sung with a raucous bounce.) Just as Dietrich leaves the stage, the band and chorus launch into a 1917 number called 'In Grandma's Day They Never Did the Fox-trot', which came from a London show called *Zig-Zag*. (Since nothing in any Hitchcock movie is without its significance, it would be interesting to know exactly what special attraction this song held for the director.)

In *No Highway* there was no opportunity for Dietrich to sing and because almost the entire action takes place in the cabin of an airliner, she has only one outfit to show off in, although she does appear briefly in different frocks in the final scenes. For most of the film Dietrich is wearing a plain wool dress, but over it she wears a Balmain mink cape, with a fur stole used as a collar. Later she said, 'I have no fur coats. I haven't the courage any more. To buy a fur coat for $10,000 I must earn at least ten times that much. Who cares? All these stories about my buying mink stoles to wear on top of mink coats. Did I really do that? Stories grow and grow. But if I did it was for the screen – one mink coat looks nothing on the screen – not to wear in bed.' (In *Desire* she wears a mink in bed.)

The story of the mink capes has been confirmed by the manageress of Balmain, Ginette Spanier, who became a close friend of Dietrich's. Madame Spanier recalled how, at 10 a.m. one day, a *vendeuse* came into her office and announced that Marlene Dietrich was in the fitting-room, trying on mink coats. 'I laughed. It was so unlikely. A typical couture joke, so I said, "That will do, go back to your work." "Mais c'est vrai, madame," the girl kept saying. I went to see for myself. There she stood: blonde, pale, beautiful beyond words, smileless, draped in our £4,000 mink cape.' (£4,000 in 1951 was an enormous amount of money.) Dietrich said that she found the cape 'rather poor', so Madame Spanier sent for the longest mink stole they could find, which she then draped around as a collar. Spanier analysed Dietrich's style: 'Choice is easy for her. She thinks out a whole wardrobe in terms of her various appearances. She even sees her social life in terms of star appearances . . . Marlene is intelligent, ruthless and quite extraordinary over clothes.' Spanier also said that at times she had to quell the outrage of her staff, who were often obliged to start a dress more than six times before Dietrich was satisfied. What interest could the audience have in a *seam*, Spanier wondered? And if they did have time to notice something as detailed as that, she surmised that the picture would be a flop anyway. But Dietrich was not to be put off, and pointed out that with the advent of the big screen everything was magnified even further. 'If, in twenty-five years, Maria, my daughter, sees the picture and notices the seam all puckered she will say, "How could Mother have stood such a thing?" '

'I dress for the image,' Dietrich told Cynthia Kee. 'Not for myself, not for the public, not for fashion, not for men. The image? A conglomeration of all the parts I've ever played on the screen.'

As the 1950s progressed Dietrich's image became more and more remote from the character that people might have expected to see on the screen. Her next Hollywood film, Fritz Lang's *Rancho Notorious* – a 'lousy movie' she calls it today – was also her last stab at the role of the saloon-bar hostess that had begun with *Destry*. Like many of Lang's other films, *Rancho Notorious* is deceptively conventional in western terms, but is in fact riddled with symbolism and film-noir humour. The character of Altar Keane – Dietrich's role – became, in Richard Whitehall's assessment, 'a flaming vision . . . one of the most gorgeous collections of snapshots to have been assembled together' in one film. First glimpsed astride a cowboy on all fours in a bar-room obstacle race, Dietrich passes from ragged Victorian finery through corseted cheesecake to traditional wild-west jeans, jerkin and cowboy shirt. For her one song – 'Get Away, Young Man, Get Away', with the punch line '*If* you can' – she wears a black dress that is 'more a feat of engineering than an example of haute-couture', as Whitehall wrote. In the final death scene that Dietrich ever did, she is shot by the avenging anti-hero, played by Arthur Kennedy. Dietrich, who had known Lang for years, was distressed by his technique of pacing out exactly where he wanted the actors to move and making chalk marks on the floor. As his legs were longer than hers, every movement proved difficult for Dietrich. Nevertheless, the very things for which the film was criticized – obviously painted sets, the lurid colours and an unbelievably melodramatic plot – now add to its appeal as an example of the baroque western. To all intents and purposes, *Rancho Notorious* was Dietrich's farewell to the old-style Hollywood star vehicle; her main role from 1953 onwards was as that endlessly engrossing character, Marlene Dietrich.

Early in 1953, Dietrich's daughter was helping to organize a charity gala circus at Madison Square Gardens in New York. Dietrich decided that she didn't want to be seen riding on an elephant, but agreed to play the ringmaster. Dressed in top hat, white tie, tail-coat, black silk tights and riding boots, cracking the whip she made her first appearance in American vaudeville. Predictably, it caused a sensation, and led to her engagement in the cabaret at the Sahara Hotel in Las Vegas. Having so often played cabaret singers – from Lola-Lola onwards – it was inevitable that Dietrich should eventually become one. In addition to a repertory of songs from her movies and records, and some numbers from her wartime concerts, she included some well-known numbers which she adapted to suit her style; these came to belong to her as much as those songs written specially for her.

Jean-Louis, the Parisian-born Hollywood designer, began making his famous series of draped, beaded, feathered and apparently transparent gowns for her, and the dresses became as much a part of her performance as the songs. Dietrich summed up his work as 'talent, knowledge, patience, kindness'. The two of them would start 'always with the material', according to Dietrich. 'We go together to these places where they import materials and pick on what we like. I know what I want to look like and he makes the dress.'

Dietrich's cabaret act became something of an institution in Las Vegas throughout the 1950s, and she had it down to a fine art. She would usually make her entrance to 'La Vie en Rose' – which she adopted as her signature tune in America (she was not allowed to sing it in France, where Edith Piaf had made it her own property) – with a wind machine gently blowing the chiffon folds of her wispy dress to tease the customers into believing that they were about to see even more of her. Then came a few songs ('Twenty minutes, they ask you to please don't do any more. They want them back to the gambling tables'), before she left the stage to change into top hat and tails. On her return she would sing a group of songs written for men. 'All the good songs have been written for men, all of them,' she told Maximilian Schell. 'That's why I put on tails.'

In 1954 she appeared at the Café de Paris in London with a version of this act (without the tails that year, although she did bring them with her for her re-engagement the following summer), and Noël Coward introduced her on the first night. 'She was wearing a dress that could only be described as a masterpiece of illusion,' wrote Milton Shulman. 'It was transparent enough to make you think you were seeing everything and opaque enough to make you realize you were seeing nothing. Houdini must have designed it.'

According to Kathleen Tynan's biography of her husband, Kenneth Tynan disappeared for three days after having made Dietrich's acquaintance; he spent this time with Dietrich: 'Ken would go backstage after her performance, and Dietrich would shoot out a hand from her dressing-room and drag him inside, spurning other suitors.' Tynan, readdressing the Dietrich style once he had had the opportunity to become personally acquainted with it, concluded: 'Life with its hands on its hips and its chin looking for a right-hook. Yet soft withall as yielding as quicksand and as perilous. London has never suffered at the hands of so compassionate a murderess. May we rest in peace.'

When she was not being the 'world's most glamorous grandmother' – wheeling her daughter's family through Central Park – or reasserting her status on stage, Dietrich returned to the film studio a few more times. She played a brief barroom scene in Mike Todd's *Around the World in 80 Days*, and was beautifully costumed by Jean Louis for a wan comedy, *The Monte Carlo Story*, her only Italian-made film, which was memorable for her crooning 'Way Back Home in Indiana'.

Dietrich narrowly missed being nominated for one of the Academy Awards that she has said she so despises for her double role in *Witness for the Prosecution*. It had to be kept a secret that she played the Cockney charwoman as well as the unfriendly witness so as not to spoil the tension for the public.

In 1958 Dietrich joined a distinguished cast to play Tanya, the cigar-smoking Madame of the bordertown cathouse, in Orson Welles's *Touch of Evil*, which was her own favourite among her later roles. Dietrich worshipped Welles. She was fascinated by the art of editing, and had a deep admiration for directors who could transcend the medium of the commercial cinema to achieve some artistic truth. Nowadays she says of him, 'He was a genius and we all worked for him for nothing; people should cross themselves when they say his name.' Welles himself declared, 'For me, almost everything that's called "directing" is a great bluff. . . The only "direction" of any importance is exercised in the process of editing.' Dietrich's scenes were all shot in one night; she prepared her own costume and turned up on the set made up in her black wig. Welles at first did not recognize her and walked right past, then turned and let out a whoop of pleasure. Welles's own role, as the crooked and repulsive policeman Quinlan, had a sympathetic side to it, 'because of something quite different I've given him,' Welles said, 'the fact that he's been able to love Marlene Dietrich, that he's taken a bullet intended for his friend . . .'

Even Welles could not separate Dietrich from the character he had created for her. *Variety*'s reviewer concluded, 'Miss Dietrich is rather sultry and fun to watch, even though it's somewhat incongruous to see her walk into the Mexican darkness at the picture's finish, turn to wave, then wail "Adios".' In his essay about the film in *Cahiers du Cinéma* (the prime Welles-worship journal in the world), François Truffaut didn't bother to mention Dietrich at all but found it 'a magical film that makes us think of fairy tales . . . a film which humbles us a bit because it's by a man who thinks more swiftly than we do.'

Welles was in the audience to see Dietrich make her first stage appearance in France in December 1959. At the Théâtre de l'Étoile she ordered that the first few rows of stalls be removed, so that the audience would see her lit correctly with the by now ritualized lighting scheme by Jo Davis.She presented her latest groups of songs, with a double-quick change out of the spangles and feathers to the top hat and tails.

Noël Coward was on hand, and commented in his diary, 'Marlene is a fabulous success. She looks ravishing and tears the place up. Privately I didn't like anything she did except "One for my baby". She has developed a hard, brassy assurance and she belts out every song harshly and without finesse. All her aloof, almost lazy glamour has been overlaid by a noisy, "take-this-and-like-it" method which, to me, is disastrous.' Coward did not understand; he had relaxed already into the Indian summer of his career, but Dietrich was bidding for a place in the new decade. While contemporaries like Joan Crawford, Bette Davis and Tallulah Bankhead were being offered roles in which they wore fright wigs, blacked out the odd tooth and became the stars of a series of horror-story movies, Dietrich was about to take centre stage as one of the creators of sixties taste.

THE NEW LOOK

Christian Dior provided Dietrich's wardrobe for *Stage Fright*, *opposite* with Jane Wyman, and *No Highway*. The skirt length well below the knee, the nipped-in waist and the buttons down the back were all key elements in the New Look. Although eventually Dietrich's allegiance remained with Balenciaga and Chanel, she was associated in the public eye with the house of Dior because of these films. She later paid back the compliment in her walk-on appearance in *Paris When It Sizzles*, in which she was filmed getting out of a giant white Rolls-Royce and darting into the Dior headquarters.

So Lang

Hollywood seemed not to know what to do with the Dietrich of the 1950s. The industry was in the first stage of its decade-long crisis as the domination of television became apparent. *Rancho Notorious* was more or less a replay of the theme of *Destry Rides Again*, played partly in flashback to allow Dietrich to appear as a younger version of the character of Altar Keene. It was directed by Fritz Lang, whom she came to loathe as a director. This was all the more odd because they had once been friends. The film is a riot of Technicolor 1950s kitsch, but at the time was a clear dead end for Dietrich. Her search for a new outlet – radio having provided only partial satisfaction – led her to the sensational appearances in Las Vegas that created her second American career. She celebrated her fifty-third birthday in her ringmaster's outfit, joining the strings in a serenade. From 1954 onwards her screen career took second place to her *métier* as a cabaret entertainer; the top hat and tails, worn, *opposite*, at the 'April in Paris' ball in New York, became as much a symbol of her style as the tights and high-heels had once been.

I Wish You Love

When Dietrich's daughter, Maria Riva, gave birth to her first child Dietrich became for the press 'the world's most glamorous grandmother', and remained so for the next twenty years. Maria herself had a successful career as a television actress and Dietrich increasingly relied upon her as adviser, and later as companion for her tours. The transition from little girl in Berlin to sophisticated theatre personality cannot have been easy for Maria. They are seen, *opposite*, at Gertrude Lawrence's funeral in New York in 1952. Much later, when Dietrich sang the English translation of Charles Trenet's 'Que Reste-t-il de Nos Amours' it was 'as a love song sung to a child'.

CAFÉ DE PARIS

Dietrich credited Noël Coward with having persuaded her to make her first foray into cabaret in Europe, which took place at the then still chic Café de Paris, off Piccadilly Circus in London. On the first night

Coward introduced her with his rhyme – preserved for posterity on her celebrated recording – which ends:

Though we all might enjoy,
Seeing Helen of Troy
As a gay, cabaret, entertainer
I doubt that she could
Be one quarter as good
As our legendary, lovely,
Marlene.

MARLENE DIETRICH
appearing at the
CAFÉ DE PARIS
LONDON, W I

NETWORK

Rehearsing for one of her
broadcasts of the radio serial
Café Istanbul in New York. The
hat with veil, so fashionable in
the early 1950s, had long been
part of Dietrich's style. In some
of her films, *Dishonored*

*overleaf, above right, Seven
Sinners, overleaf, left,* and *The
Lady is Willing, overleaf, below
right,* veils found their way into
the plot, and in her new role as
a demure grandmother Dietrich
may have found it convenient
to look somewhat matronly
from time to time. *page 118*

A Lighter Shade of Pale

Although she seemed to enjoy advising other women to wear grey, navy and black, Dietrich herself nearly always wore white or beige, especially when travelling. She had probably learnt that a light-coloured outfit made a better photograph for her *bêtes noires*, the freelance photographers, who were in constant pursuit, whether she was in Rome, London, or in the unlikely location of Blackpool.

PERFECT AUDIENCE

One of the pleasures of no longer living in Hollywood was the theatre: Dietrich attended the sensational début of Maria Callas in the title role of *Norma* at the Met in 1956, *above, right*. She is also seen with Judy Garland after her famous solo at the Palace, *opposite*; with Mary Martin, Dietrich's replacement as Kurt Weill's Venus, *above*; and with Jean Cocteau and the Begum Aga Khan at the Paris Opéra for the première of Gilbert Bécaud's *Opéra d'Aran*, *right*.

1297-

STUDY IN LEATHER

Kenneth Tynan called Dietrich 'the Venus with black leather in her voice'. Since *Dishonored*, *opposite*, she had learnt of the allure and the comfort of leather. On the set of *Witness for the Prosecution*, *below*, Tyrone Power and Charles Laughton sit waiting for their cues, and Dietrich's gesture seems suitably authoritative. To go with another all-black leather jump suit, Dietrich had a pale coat lined in lamb, *left*. 'It's the only thing that will keep me warm in New York,' she said. 'Who could be bored with a leather coat lined with lamb?'

PURSUIT OF PERFECTION

Dietrich's first studio recording
for an LP record, which
included not only old wartime
favourites like 'Lili Marlene', but
also 'The Surrey with a Fringe
on Top' sung in German.

No longer a movie star, but
an independent force in the
world of cabaret and theatre,
Dietrich faces the 1960s with
confidence.

5

DIETRICH

The stage lights dim on the band which has been playing a loud medley comprising 'La Vie en Rose', 'The Boys in the Backroom' and 'Falling in Love Again'. There is no drumroll, no fanfare. A polite voice over the loudspeaker system announces, 'Ladies and gentlemen: Miss Marlene Dietrich.' A hand grabs the stage curtain and hurls it aside; there is a flash of sparkling sequins, a flurry of swansdown feathers, and Dietrich appears – the blonde wig slightly tousled over her right eye, the spotlights making her lipgloss sparkle. She wears a look of amazement that the audience should be applauding – just for this? – and gives a smile, perhaps even a conspiratorial wink to an imaginary friend in the stalls. Her voice booms through the mike as she sings 'I Can't Give You Anything But Love', or maybe 'Gonna Take a Sentimental Journey', or the old stand-by 'Look Me Over Closely'.

Sometimes the sequins were silver, sometimes gold or pink. The swansdown wrap might on occasion have been replaced by an evening coat of paillettes, but the formula remained pretty much the same: after five or six songs she would exit, take off the wrap, and return looking vulnerable and serious instead of bold and brassy, as she had for 'The Laziest Gal in Town'. For this more serious part of the show even the jokes were discarded, including the comment that always got a laugh in England, 'American men must be the most romantic men in the world.' Instead she would announce, speaking the words softly as if giving a testimony:

> It isn't by chance, I happen to be
> A *femme fatale*, the toast of Paris,
> For over the talk, the chatter and smoke
> I'm good for a laugh, a drink and a joke.

This sad ballad, 'The World Was Young' (which had also been sung by Piaf, Pearl Bailey and Eartha Kitt), introduced the main section of Dietrich's *tour de chant*, as she perfected it in the 1960s – that unjustly maligned decade of which she became, somewhat to the surprise of her critics and friends, a part of 'the scene'. At her show at the Théâtre de l'Étoile, Dietrich was accompanied by Burt Bacharach, as she had been for her last appearances in Las Vegas. What von Sternberg had done for her in the 1930s, Bacharach achieved in the 1960s. Dietrich's movies had provided her with a framework in which to display the art of her personal volte-face; in her cabaret acts Bacharach enabled her to present a series of statements to the audience – through the juxtaposing of certain songs, or in the introductions to them. The effect was to make the audience believe that the person they were watching was the 'real' Dietrich.

The characteristics Dietrich displayed on stage included professionalism, glamour and nostalgia, all of which were implicit in the way she arranged her songs to start the evening and in her choice of costume. Her garments, though timeless, often seemed to make reference to the past of her films and, in the case of her slinky, beaded gown, to those far-fetched designs that had once been the work of Travis Banton. As the show progressed, she would begin to send the whole thing up with a touch of self-deprecating humour. Later, in a serious mood, she would offer a lesson in love. 'This is a song of goodbye and of tears and of long parting' was her announcement before she sang a song made famous by Richard Tauber, 'Frag Nicht Warum'. This became, for Harold Hobson, something 'moving and gallant', and in his opinion her singing of the eighteenth-century American folksong 'Go 'Way from My Window' expressed 'the height and depth of love by catching it with infallible precision in the very moment of its defeat'. As well as these songs of the past, she sang modern songs about love. 'Marie-Marie' by Gilbert Bécaud is the letter of a prisoner writing to his lover and describing to her the daily routine of the jail – from his work in the library to the fish he eats on Fridays. Her hands clasped behind her back, as if bound, Dietrich's voice used to break on the word 'vendredi', and suddenly struggling free – her one gesture – she would fling out her right arm in a yearning plea for freedom. Her voice was just as expressive for Charles Trenet's 'Que Reste-t-il de Nos Amours?' (translated into English as 'I Wish You Love'); she sang 'With my best/My very best/I set you free', with gentle chiding, 'as a love song sung to a child'.

For the benefit of her young audience, and to the surprise of some of her own generation, a strongly pacifist element emerged during the course of her recital, both in her presentation of the old marching song 'Lili Marlene' and in her choice of ballads; these included Bob Dylan's 'Blowin' in the Wind'; the Australian song about the soldier returning from war to find his home and family gone – 'White Grass'; and most famously Pete Seeger's 'Where Have All the Flowers Gone?' This song had already been recorded by an American group, and by Seeger himself, but when Dietrich introduced it into her repertory, first in French, then German, and finally English, it became her most famous number. Bacharach scored it beautifully, starting with a single guitar and gradually bringing in all the orchestra until, at the line 'Gone to graveyards every one', Dietrich's vehement crescendo was echoed by the orchestra which then died away, leaving the solo guitar for her reprise of the first stanza. This song always appeared last on the programme, and was sung with a single spotlight on her face; the rest of the stage was in darkness – a daring effect which even in the largest theatres achieved the effect of a close-up on the screen.

Back on stage, there would be curtain call after curtain call. Dietrich, if she gave encores, was sparing with them. Before finally singing 'Falling in Love Again' ('the inevitable one'), she would give an announcement: 'And now I want you to meet a man whom I love and admire. I've loved and admired him for a long time, but the more I'm allowed to work with him, the more I admire him. I can't love him any more than I love him now. He's my conductor, my arranger, he's my teacher, he's my critic and I wish I could say he was my composer. But that isn't true, he's everybody's composer. He has written so many hit songs and you know them all and his name is Burt! . . . Bacharach!'

In 1964 Dietrich told Derek Prouse, 'I sing the songs I like to sing. I have no script and no director. I don't have to waste my energy explaining why I want something like this and not like that. I don't have to fight with anybody or say "Please let me do this" . . . I stand or fall by my own decisions. No front office interference; just my conductor Burt Bcharach and me.'

Bacharach came into Dietrich's life by chance. Peter Matz, until then her regular accompanist, had been 'borrowed' by Noël Coward and Matz sent Bacharach over to meet Dietrich in Beverly Hills. Dietrich told Kathleen Tynan, 'Burt insists to this day that he didn't change me. That's not true. When he walked in the first time he said: "I don't like you to start like that. [It was with 'Look Me Over Closely'.] How would you like to swing it?" So we did.' Together they toured the world. They made four albums,

Dietrich in Rio, *Wiedersehen mit Marlene*, *Die Neue Marlene* and *Dietrich in London*, but their best achievement on record was a session in Paris in 1962 that included 'Where Have All the Flowers Gone', 'Marie-Marie' and Jacques Prévert's poem 'Déjeuner du Matin'. For this last song they used the arrangement by Josef Kosma. Like Dietrich, he was an old habitué of Berlin; he had studied with Eisler and had left for Paris in 1933. With this beautiful song, in which the singer describes one by one the gestures of the man who eventually leaves, 'Sans me parler, sans me regarder', Dietrich achieves the perfect balance between speech and song, and Bacharach's languorous orchestration complements her voice perfectly. The rest of the session comprised Salvador's 'Cherche la Rose' and 'The World Was Young', which she sang in German.

Accompanied by Bacharach, Dietrich undertook the most controversial and stormy engagement of her career when she agreed to go to Germany for a series of concerts in the spring and summer of 1960. Her contract was for appearances in Berlin, Munich, Hamburg, Düsseldorf, Frankfurt and Cologne. As soon as the tour was announced a slur campaign began in the German press protesting the return of the 'traitress'. Dietrich told a columnist at the *New York Herald Tribune*, Art Buchwald, 'They offered me a guaranteed £1,500 a performance, more money than I've been paid anywhere, including Las Vegas. I assumed that if they were willing to pay that kind of money the Germans wanted to see me. Now the German papers are bringing up all the old things. They say I wore an American uniform during the war, which I did.' The papers asserted that she had also worn a French uniform in the celebrations in Paris in 1955, which she denied: 'I did march and I did rekindle the flame over the Tomb of the Unknown Soldier, but I was wearing an American Legion hat and a blue raincoat.' One German headline proclaimed, 'Marlene Dietrich says she can't forget Hitler'. Dietrich replied simply, 'Who can?'

In front of the theatre in Berlin on her first night a picket-line formed, holding placards that declared 'Go home, Marlene'. There were bomb threats and the fear of demonstrations. 'I'm not afraid of my reception as a performer. My act has gone over wherever it has played. But I hate to be involved in politics.' Dietrich added that the one thing she did have a fear of was someone throwing an egg and hitting her famous swansdown coat. 'If an egg ever hits it I don't know what I'll do. You couldn't clean it in a million years.' Instead of ending the Berlin performance with 'Falling in Love Again', she began with it. 'Now here's the other song from *The Blue Angel*,' she announced immediately after the very warm applause. Silence ensued. 'Have you forgotten?' Eventually someone called out 'Lola', and Dietrich smiled and said, 'Ja, die "Lola".' The tour passed uneventfully, and even had some lighter moments, such as when Hedwig Ernst, whom Dietrich calls 'a real Berlin lady', came from out of the crowd, embraced Dietrich and said, 'Can't we all be friends again?' She was received by Willi Brandt and took lunch at the old UFA studios, where *The Blue Angel* had been filmed thirty years before.

The following year Dietrich played the part of Madame Bertholdt, the widow of an executed Nazi General in Stanley Kramer's *Judgment at Nuremburg*. This film, an unusually fair-minded attempt to make clear the issues involved, concentrates on the trial of four ex-judges. Madame Bertholdt appears solely in the out-of-court scenes, where she speaks out for those who had hated Hitler but who had had to work with him. Spencer Tracy, playing the presiding judge, is not entirely believable with his all-American, gruff good humour. However, there is one particularly effective scene in which he and Dietrich walk through the streets at night and pass a beer-hall. The men inside are singing 'Lili Marlene', and Dietrich tells him how much more touching the original German words are. This has a good emotional tug to it, as has the moment when she challenges him across the coffee-cups about whether he believes that people like her knew of the atrocities. 'As far as I can find out, no one in this country knew,' he replies. Maximilian Schell, as the defence counsel, gives an impassioned performance, and among all the American actors he and Dietrich stand out with their more authentic European manner and accents.

Judgment at Nuremburg was Dietrich's last Hollywood film. Although other roles were offered – among them the lead in Enid Bagnold's *The Chalk Garden*, in which her opening line would have been 'Will you bring me my teeth, the lower set I mean. I left them on the drawing-room table' – good sense prevailed, and instead she and

Bacharach embarked on a tour of Israel. 'The tears I have cried over Germany have dried,' she later wrote. 'In Israel I washed my face in the cool waters of compassion.' She brought away with her 'Shir Hatan' – the song of the animals crying at night because they are hungry, and of the child crying at night because he is hungry and lonely. Every meeting with Dietrich became (in Ken Tynan's memorable description) for the first half-hour a tireless self-chronicle of how she had 'wowed them in Warsaw, mowed them down in Moscow, savaged them in Sydney, been pelted with poppies in Ispahan'.

After every performance the ritual outside the theatre was as much a part of the evening's entertainment as the lighting-effects or the overture. A crowd of fans would wait patiently, for it would be more than an hour before Dietrich emerged from the stage door on the arm of Burt Bacharach, or with whichever friend or member of the family was in attendance. Wearing a brocade evening suit, or a neat Chanel number, she would distribute photographs and sign autographs, silently and dutifully, writing 'Dietrich' in a large, bold scrawl across a programme, record sleeve or bank-note – whichever was proffered.

I saw her thus in 1964 on a December night in London; her hair was even blonder than on the stage, and the pink wool of her suit added a pallor to her make-up. One of those West End crones, a theatrical bag-lady, stood by the door, and only she was accorded a special greeting: a hug and kiss – the rest of the crowd was given the autographs it had come to collect. A pompous English voice tried to engage her in conversation with a question about one of her songs. She didn't look up or show that she had heard, but after a tingling pause, still signing, she simply murmured, 'Yes.' It could have been a scene from a movie.

In Sydney, Dietrich was photographed lifting her skirt and letting herself fall from a car bonnet into the arms of the gathered fans. When she appeared on Broadway for the first time in 1967, she stood right on top of the car, flinging fistfuls of photographs to the assembled crowd. All this hero-worship did not occur without a certain amount of adverse criticism. Those who drew back and regarded the phenomenon coldly might agree with Francis Wyndham in his 1964 essay:

The theatre is a place where it is difficult enough to work one illusion: Dietrich undertakes two. The first, a variation on the old mirror trick, is purely physical. Sustained by clothes, make-up, lighting and confidence, she looks beautiful, neither young nor old. The second is more ambitious and more subtle. Fixing us with her sad and serious gaze, she hypnotizes us into seeing her as holy, untouchable – who would dare to criticize a sacred rite? What she does is neither difficult nor diverting, but the fact that she does it at all fills the onlookers with wonder . . . It takes two to make a conjuring trick: the illusionist's sleight of hand and the stooge's desire to be deceived. To these necessary elements (her own technical competence and her audience's sentimentality) Marlene Dietrich adds a third – the mysterious force of her belief in her own magic. Those who find themselves unable to share this belief tend to blame themselves rather than her.

By the end of the 1960s Burt Bacharach had departed from Dietrich's entourage, and although her concerts and tours continued she said that her heart was no longer in it, that she did it just for the money. While this may have been the main reason, an important part of the spur must also have been her own apparent need for recognition and the desire that most performers have to be on the stage. She returned to Paris – to gain great acclaim at Pierre Cardin's Espace, the theatre on the Champs-Elysées – went to London twice, and toured many cities in the USA and Great Britain. On her arrival at Heathrow in 1975 for what proved to be her final tour, she confronted the press photographers and interviewers with a stony glare, and having said she didn't wish to be photographed she took a swipe at one persistent photographer and knocked his camera to the floor. The pictures of her doing this naturally made the centre-spreads of the newspapers.

If her patience with the paparazzi was exhausted, her performances in these final years took on a new and touching fragility. Whereas in the 1950s and 1960s she had nearly always refused to give any encores, and would sometimes even engage in banter with those people who called out for 'Lili Marlene' to be sung in German, or for any other number, she now sang 'Je Tire Ma Révérence' and 'I Get a Kick Out of You', taking the opportunity to salute the audience on 'You'.

In October 1975, appearing once more in Sydney, she tripped on the stage, fell, and broke her left femur. She was eventually flown to America, where she spent many months in hospital. She emerged with what she herself has described as a 'not unattractive' limp. It came as a surprise in 1978 when it was announced that she would play a role in a film again. As the elderly aristocratic procuress in David Hemmings's *Just a Gigolo*, she wears a black costume: a hat with a veil, a skirt with a slit up the side and knee-length boots – a homage to all the elements that had made up the Dietrich style of the past. On the first day of shooting she had to be escorted by two assistants who supported her on each side, but she quickly gained confidence, and commentators noted that by the third day she was striding on to the set. She half whispers, half sings the title song to the bemused-looking hero, David Bowie; she said that it was his presence alone in the film that interested her, and they shared top billing on the publicity material.

In 1979 Dietrich's autobiography, *Nehmt Nur Mein Leben*, was published in Germany; eventually it was translated into French and English. The book is not so much a 'life and times', but a monologue about loyalty and friendship and the challenge of survival. It is made up of a series of snatches – or vignettes – reminiscent of how Dietrich would take her bow at the end of the evening's recital, when she used to stand behind the curtains and pull them inwards, so that when she let go the audience would catch just a glimpse of her, standing with that practised look of mild astonishment on her face at the audience's remaining there and shouting for more.

This vigilant guard over her privacy, and a still highly professional concern with the everyday technicalities of film-making are much in evidence in the 1984 documentary *Marlene*; the programme was directed by Maximilian Schell and was subsequently nominated for an Oscar. Schell's collage of film clips and newsreels is superbly, if somewhat mischievously, juxtaposed with extracts from their taped conversation (which is reputed to be seventeen hours long). 'I'm not contracted to be exciting,' she said, and it is often more interesting to speculate why she doesn't want to talk about certain people or things than to listen to what she does say to Schell. When he suggests that the film should have a Proustian quality, she laughs, 'You'll never sell that in America,' and when, exasperated, he leaves the room in a huff she snaps, 'You should go back to Mama Schell and learn some manners.'

When the history of twentieth-century cinema is written, it is probable that other stars of the great days of Hollywood will be chosen before Dietrich as fine actresses. But no one, surely, will be able to find someone more glamorous or professional – a great performer who was happy to obey the directors with whom she had the good fortune to work, including some of the most successful the cinema has known. She was equally fortunate in her work with Schell. In 1990, talking to *Paris Match*, she said of him, 'He is an incorrigible optimist. He needed to be, for I resisted him rather than co-operate. My old aversion to speaking about myself was still the reason.'

Through all her films, recitals, interviews and books, people have sought the reason behind the success and durability of the Dietrich style. Is it because she was 'every man's mistress and mother, every woman's lover and aunt' – as she was for Kenneth Tynan? Or because, as Alice B. Toklas suggested, she was 'a warm but ordinary woman'; or perhaps (as with Hemingway) because she was 'brave, beautiful, loyal, kind and generous', her 'mystery' the result of her knowing 'more about love than anyone'?

When he introduced her first show in Paris in 1959, Jean Cocteau concluded, 'Quite obviously, one can't introduce Marlene. All the same, we can welcome her and thank her for being what she is . . . This bird of paradise, this bark in full spread of sail, this miracle of grace is a rare force, a force of active goodness . . . It would be idle to say more and abuse the honour she has done me in letting me talk to you about her. Better let her come on whose name begins with a caress and ends with a whiplash – Marlene Dietrich.'

CHANEL

'If I can't go to Paris, I wait,' said Dietrich in 1960, and she wore Chanel's latest version of the classic suit in London, *right*, in Cannes, *below*, and when arriving to view a Chanel collection in 1966, *below right*. A look that never faltered, the Chanel two-piece was the key item in Coco's comeback and vital for her grip on the modern fashion world. It was an achievement comparable in its way to Dietrich's own conquest of the modern fashion scene.

DESIGNED BY JEAN LOUIS

Dietrich often had two identical sets of costumes made – one for use in private and one for stage or screen. This brocade evening suit was designed by Jean Louis, the creator of all her stage costumes in the 1950s and 1960s; he was also the costumier for her only Italian film, *The Monte Carlo Story*, in which she first wore this favourite outfit, *overleaf*, *above*. She wore it on stage in Düsseldorf for a UNICEF concert in 1962, *right*, and for the gala opening of a tribute to Marlene Dietrich at the Museum of Modern Art in New York. Seated beside Yves Saint Laurent at Maxim's in Paris, *overleaf*, *below*, Dietrich may have had some words of comfort for this young designer who had not yet launched his own house and was still working in the shadow of Dior.

SOLANG, NOCH UNTER'N LINDEN

Dietrich's return to Germany in 1960 was the stormiest engagement of her entire stage career. She received death threats from former Nazis and declared herself afraid of nothing except eggs – because the stain would never wash out. In Berlin she presented herself in a natty array of headgear: on the plane journey *overleaf*, *right*, and to meet Willi Brandt *right*. When not confronting the only somewhat friendly press, Dietrich visited the UFA studios, where *The Blue Angel* had been filmed exactly thirty years before.

WITH THE BEATLES

Rehearsing for the final line-up at the 1963 Royal Variety Performance; the newly-famous Beatles were quite low on the bill, and were thus relegated to the second line. Dietrich, as the star of the show, is flanked by Tommy Steele and Charlie Drake, but photographers were not slow to scent a historic meeting and soon grouped her with the Fab Four. Later she wrote that she loved the Beatles and, saddened by their split, that she 'despised' the person who had brought it about. It was at this performance that London heard Dietrich sing 'Where Have All the Flowers Gone?' for the first time. Her success led to her famous engagement the following season at the Queen's Theatre, Shaftesbury Avenue, and the recital has been immortalized by her million-selling album *Dietrich in London*. Somewhat to everyone's surprise, Dietrich became one of the icons of the 1960s, along with the Beatles and James Bond (she is shown here with Sean Connery on the set of *A Fine Madness*).

SIXTIES PEOPLE

Nureyev, Dietrich declared, was the most arrogant person she had ever met. Backstage at the Palais des Sports in Paris she wears the inevitable Chanel suit with that essential 1960s accessory, knee-high boots. In the 1930s, Dietrich had been conspicuous in such footwear, *opposite*, *above left*, but by the 1960s she was just part of the international booted brigade.

AND HIS NAME IS . . .

At every performance they gave together, Dietrich paid homage to Burt Bacharach, whom she called 'my teacher, my accompanist, my critic'. In the front row for Nat King Cole's opening night at the Olympia in Paris in 1960, Dietrich is radiant in the company of her arranger. Just as von Sternberg had been the man she wished to please most in the 1930s, so in the 1960s she said that the applause and the success meant little to her, and that her 'highest goal' was to please Bacharach.

Ou Sont les Fleurs?

Dietrich first sang Pete Seeger's pacifist ballad in Paris. In 1962 she returned here to star at the Olympia music hall and was greeted by Gilbert Bécaud, *below*, whose ballad 'Marie-Marie' was a feature of Dietrich's first studio recording session for many years. At the age of sixty Dietrich's awareness of just how far she could go had never been stronger; she had a softer hairline and fuller lips. And in the sixties she took to the miniskirt, with the occasional unusual result, *overleaf*.

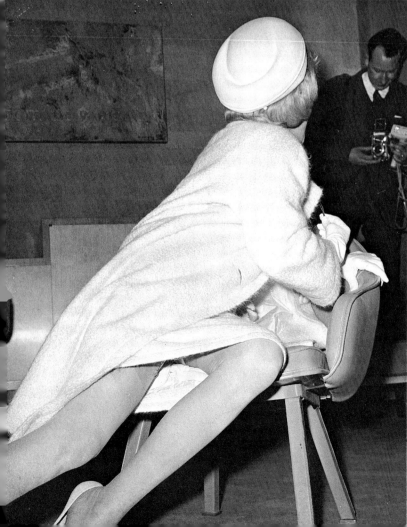

OLYMPIA '62

Even when Dietrich was in her sixties, her figure coped with the rigorous demands that Jean Louis's wardrobe placed on it, not to mention the unflattering attentions of the camera during rehearsals at the Olympia in Paris, *right* and *overleaf*. Noël Coward said of this performance, 'I have never seen her so good.' Bruno Coquatrix, the impresario of the Olympia, was at this time said to be the only man who could persuade Dietrich to perform in Europe. She rehearsed for weeks, including a session with composer Henri Salvador and his wife, who had written 'Cherche la Rose' for her.

THE LAST TOURS

Arriving at the stage door of the Theatre Royal, Drury Lane, 1971, with the faithful Maria in attendance. This was Dietrich's first performance in London for several years and it proved that she had not lost her power over a huge and enthusiastic midnight audience. A young man, delirious with enthusiasm, took off his dinner jacket and flung it on to the stage, whereupon she promptly picked it up and put it on, hands on her hips, a red carnation stuck behind one ear, the sequins shooting off sparks. Benny Green later wrote, 'A thorn in the side of time – how had she managed to smuggle her looks across into the 1970s?'. *Below right:* On stage in Sydney, where her career was halted, she picks up a Digger's hat. The streamers, the flowers, the applause, all were finally done.

6

THE RECORDED LEGACY: DISCOGRAPHY

Dietrich's recording career lasted exactly fifty years; her first discs were made in Berlin in 1928 and the last was the soundtrack album for *Just a Gigolo* in 1978. From the high-voiced, piping, Berlinese 'snotty' youngster (as she calls herself) to the deep-toned *diseuse* of the great concerts of the 1950s and 1960s, she covered a wide repertory and recorded several numbers six or seven times. In the case of Holländer's 'Johnny', for instance, of which five versions exist, it is fascinating to see not only how she stuck to the same basic phrasing, but also how her long-rehearsed timing and the nuances of her recitation of 'Um, halb, vier' gained in confidence.

Her early recordings had a wide circulation in Europe; among them, 'Allein in einer Grossen Stadt' and 'Assez' achieved cult status even before World War II. Her American recordings made in the 1940s have often been reissued. These include the series made in English for Decca, and the Columbia series in German, which arose out of her broadcasts for the overseas wartime propaganda machine.

Dietrich had a substantial career on radio in the USA in the 1930s, '40s and '50s, and in addition made a few isolated European broadcasts in the 1960s. However, very little of this material has yet found its way on to disc (with the exception of three LPs). With a career as long and varied as Dietrich's, it is more than likely that other records exist that are not listed here, although some of these may be merely different compilations of previously issued items, or reissues of old material.

The catalogue numbers given in the discography usually refer to the first issue, whether it was in Europe or the USA, and no attempt has been made to chart the immense number of variant catalogue numbers that have followed over the decades. Where no matrix number is known, none is given. Dietrich's own verdict is that *Marlene Singt Berlin* is her 'best record'.

When she appeared as a guest on the celebrated BBC Radio programme *Desert Island Discs* on 4 January 1965, having chosen recordings by Stravinsky, Richter, Bernstein and Bacharach, she was asked if she was going to choose one of her own. She replied certainly not, that she had never known a painter who enjoyed looking at his own paintings, nor a writer who enjoyed reading his own books – so why should she want to listen to her own recordings?

DISCOGRAPHY

78 r.p.m. records

Berlin, June 1928
BL 4231–1 Wenn die Beste Freundin (Spoliansky–Schiffer) *Electrola EG 892*
CL 4214–2 Pot-Pourri from Es Liegt in der Luft (Spoliansky-Schiffer) *Electrola EH 146*

On the above records, Dietrich is joined on the first by Margo Lion and Oskar Karlweis; on the two sides of the selection, the three of them are joined by Käte Lenz, Otto Wallburg, Ida Wüst and Hubert von Meyerninck

Berlin, January 1930
Accompanied by the composer Friedrich Holländer and his Jazzsymphonikern
BLR 6034–2 Falling in Love Again (Holländer-Connelly) *HMV B 3524*
BLR 6035–2 Nimm Dich in Acht vor Blonden Frauen (Holländer-Rillo) *Electrola EG 1770*
BLR 6036–2 Blonde Women (Holländer) *HMV B 3524*

Berlin, February 1930
BLR 6078 Ich Bin die Fesche Lola (Holländer-Liebmann) *Electrola EG 1802*
BLR 6079–2 Lola (Holländer-Connelly) *Vic 22593*
BLR 6080–2 Kinder, Heut' Abend Such' Ich Mir 'Was Aus *Electrola EG 1802*
BLR 6129–2 Ich Bin von Kopf bis Fuss auf Liebe Eingestellt (Holländer-Liebmann) *Electrola EG 1770*
BLR 6130–1 Wenn Ich Mir 'Was Wünschen Dürfte (Holländer) *Electrola EG 2265*
BLR 1–1 This Evening, Children *7EG 8275*

The final item, the English-language version of 'Kinder, Heut' Abend', was unissued until early 1958

Berlin, 11 March 1931
16310 Peter (Nelson-Holländer) *Polydor 522751*
16311–1 Johnny, Wenn Du Geburtstag Hast (Holländer) *Polydor 522751*
16311–2 Johnny (Holländer) *Ultraphone AP 249*

Berlin, 12 March 1931
OD 250–3 Leben Ohne Liebe Kannst Du Nicht (Spoliansky-Gilbert) *Electrola EG 2285*

Berlin, 27 March 1931
OD 291–2 Quand l'Amour Meurt (Crémieux) *Electrola EG 2775*
OD 292–1 Give Me the Man (Robin-Hajos) *EG 2775*

Paris, 12 July 1933
Accompanied by the Wal-Berg Orchestra, conducted by Peter Kreuder
6465 1/2 bkp Assez (Wal-Berg-Stern-Tranchant) *Polydor 530000*
6465 4/4 bkp Assez (Wal-Berg-Stern-Tranchant) *Decca M. 452*

Paris, 15 July 1933
6469 3/4 bkp Moi, Je M'Ennuie (Wal-Berg-Francois) *Polydor 530000*
6470 bkp Ja So Bin Ich (Stolz-Reisch) *Polydor 524182*

Paris, 19 July 1933
6476 3/4 bkp Allein, in einer Grossen Stadt (Waschmann-Kolpe) *Polydor 530001*
6471 4/4 bkp Mein Blondes Baby (Kreuder-Rotter) *Polydor 530001*
6477 3/4 bkp Wo Ist der Mann? (Kreuder-Kolpe) *Polydor 47199*

Hollywood, 1935
B 1972 If It Isn't Pain, It Isn't Love (Rainger-Robin) *Decca*
B 1973 Three Sweethearts Have I (Ranger-Robin) *Decca*

Los Angeles, 11 December 1939
Accompanied by Victor Young and his orchestra
DLA 1882–B I've Been in Love Before (Holländer-Loesser) *Decca 23139*
DLA 1883–A You've Got That Look (Holländer-Loesser) *Decca 23140*
DLA 1884–C Falling in Love Again (Holländer-Connelly-Winstrom) *Decca 23141*

Los Angeles, 19 December 1939
Accompanied by Victor Young and his orchestra
DLA 1911–B The Boys in the Backroom (Holländer-Loesser) *Decca 23141*
DLA 1912–A You Go to My Head (Coots-Gillespie) *Decca 23140*
DLA 1913–A You Do Something to Me (Cole Porter) *Decca 23139*

Los Angeles, 1944
Accompanied by orchestra directed by Charles Magnante
W 730321 Lili Marlene (Leip-Schultze-Park-Davis) *Decca 23456*
W 73032 Symphonie (Alstone-Tabet-Bernstein-Lawrence) *Decca 23456*

Los Angeles, 1948
W 74700 Illusions (Holländer) *Decca A 24582*
W 74701 Black Market (Holländer) *Decca A 24582*

Co 47215 Schlitternfahrt (The Surrey with the Fringe on Top) (Rodgers-Hammerstein) *Co SV 145*
Co 47216–2 Ach Fräulein Annie Wohnt Lange Nicht Mehr Hier (Young-Burke-Spina-Metzl) *Co DC 617; Co DW 5279*
Co 47217 Lili Marlene (Schultze) *Co DC 629*
Co 47218 Taking a Chance on Love (Latouche-Fetter-Duke-Metzl) *Co DC 629*
Co 47219 Ich Hab' die Ganze Nacht Geweint (I Couldn't Sleep a Wink All Night) (Adamson-McHugh-Metzl) *Co DW 5230; Co DC 601*
Co 47220 Mean to Me *Co 4–88*
Co 47220–2 Sei Lieb zu Mir (Turk-Albert-Metzl) *Co DW 5230*
Co 47221 Time on My Hands (Adamson-Gordon-Youmans) *Co 490–G*
Co 47222–2 Miss Otis Regrets (Mein Mann ist Verhindert) (Cole Porter) *Co DW 5279*
Co 47401 Too Old to Cut the Mustard *Co 39 812**
Co 47449 Come Rain or Come Shine *Co 39 797*
Co 47448 Love Me *Co 39 797*
Co 47455–2 Good for Nothin' (Engvick-Wilder) *Co DW 5187; 39 812**
Co 48840 Time for Love *Co 39 959*
Co 48841 Look Me Over Closely (Gilkyson) *Co 39 959*

aa 21057 Dot's Nice-Donna Fight (Showalter) *PH 21 057**
aa 21057 It's the Same (Forrest-Wright) *PH 21 057**
aa 21618 Ich Hab' Noch einen Koffer in Berlin (Pinelli-Siegel) *PH 21 618*
aa 21618 Peter (Holländer) *PH 21 618*
aa1–1 Besides *PB 314**
aa1–1 Land, Sea and Air *PB 314**

*Duets with Rosemary Clooney

45 r.p.m. records

Los Angeles, 1958
EPMD 40328–IC I May Never Go Home Anymore (Roberts-Brooks) *RE-D 1146*
EPMD 40328–IC Kisses Sweeter than Wine (Newman-Campbell) *RE-D 1146*
EPMD 40329–IC Another Spring, Another Love (Shayne-Paris) *RE-D 1146*
EPMD 40329–IC Near You (Craig-Goehl) *RE-D 1146*

Paris, 12 May 1962
7 TLA 1593–21 Marie-Marie (Bécaud) *7 EGF 597*
7 TLA 1593–21 Déjeuner du Matin (Kosma-Prévert) *7 EGF 597*
7 TLA 1592–21 Où Sont les Fleurs? (Seeger-Lemarque-Rouzaud) *7 EGF 597*
7 TLA 1592–21 Cherche la Rose (Salvador) *7 EGF 597*
– Die Welt War Jung (Philippe-Gerards/Colpet) *Electrola 22180*
– Sag Mir, Wo die Blumen Sind (Seeger/Colpet) *Electrola 22180*

1964
BLY 60394–B Kleine Treue Nachtigall (Message to Martha) (Kolpe-Bacharach) *Barclay 60394 B*
BLY 60394–A Bitte Geh' Nicht Fort (Ne Me Quitte Pas) (Kolpe-Brel) *Barclay 60394 A*

London, 1965
7XEA 21168 Where Have All the Flowers Gone? (Seeger) *(EMI) POP 1379*
7XEA 21169 Blowin' in the Wind (Dylan) *(EMI) POP 1379*
MSV 6909 If He Swing by the String (Addison-Moore) *London HLR 9883*
MSV 6910 Such Trying Times (Addison-Moore) *London HLR 9883 (issued May 1964)*
– Candles Glowing (Bader-Harrison) *Pye 7N 17238*
– This World of Ours (Debout-Colpet) *Pye 7N 17238*

Berlin, 1978
7YCA–33401 Just a Gigolo (Casucci-Caesar) *Columbia DB 9050*

33 r.p.m. records

Lili Marlene
Side One: Lili Marlene (Leip-Schultze)/ Mean to Me (Turk-Albert; German lyrics, Metzl)/The Hobellied (Kreutzer) / Annie Doesn't Live Here Any More (Young-Burke-Spina; German lyrics, Metzl)/ You Have My Heart (Du Liegst Mir im Herzen)/ The Surrey with the Fringe on Top (Rodgers-Hammerstein; German lyrics, Metzl)
Side Two: Time on My Hands (Adamson-Gordon-Youmans; German lyrics, Metzl)/ Taking a Chance on Love (Latouche-Fetter-Duke; German lyrics, Metzl)/ Must I Go (Muss I Denn)/Miss Otis Regrets (Cole Porter; German lyrics, Metzl)/ You Have Taken My Soul (Du Hast die Seele Mein)/ I Couldn't Sleep a Wink Last Night (Adamson-McHugh; German lyrics, Metzl)

The original issue of this recording – Dietrich's first LP – was as a 12″ LP (Columbia GL 105) and as a set of 7″ 45 r.p.m. records (GL 4–17)

London, 21 June 1954
Marlene Dietrich at the Café de Paris (Introduced by Noël Coward)
Accompanied by George Smith and his orchestra
Side One: La Vie en Rose (Piaf-Louiguy)/ Boys in the Backroom (Loesser-Holländer)/ Lola (Liebmann-Holländer)/ Look Me Over Closely (Gilkyson/ Don't Ask Me Why (Young-Stolz-Reisch-Robinson)
Side Two: The Laziest Gal in Town (Cole Porter)/ Go 'Way from My Window (John Jacob Niles)/ Lili Marlene (Connor-Turner-Schultze)/ Falling in Love Again (Holländer-Connelly)

Matrix number: AA 07684 1R and 2R; catalogue number: BBR 8006
The American pressing of the above record includes two extra numbers: 'Lazy Afternoon' and 'No love, No Nothin''

The Copacobana Palace, Rio de Janeiro, 17 August 1959
Musical direction by Burt Bacharach

Dietrich in Rio
Side One: Look Me Over Closely (Gilkyson)/ You're the Cream in My Coffee (De Sylva-Brown-Henderson)/ My Blue Heaven (Whiting-Donaldson)/ The Boys in the Backroom (Loesser-Holländer)/ Das Lied Is Aus (Frag Nicht Warum) (Reisch-Robinson-Stolz)/ Je Tire Ma Révérence (P. Bastia)/ Well All Right (Gerald-Calhoun-Nugetre)
Side Two: Makin' Whoopee! (Kahn/Donaldson)/ I've Grown Accustomed to Her Face (Loewe-Lerner)/ One for My Baby (Arlen)/ I Will Come Back Again (G. Giltnan-K. Vannah)/ Luar do Sertao (Cearense)

Matrix numbers: 52077–A and 52077–B

Berlin and Cologne, August 1960

Wiedersehen mit Marlene: Marlene Dietrich in Deutschland
Side One: Ich Bin von Kopf bis Fuss auf Liebe Eingestellt (Holländer)/ Ich Bin die Fesche Lola (Holländer-Liebmann)/ Wer Wird denn Weinen (Hirsch-Rebner)/ Mein Blondes Baby (Kreuder)/ Peter (Nelson-Holländer)/ Allein (Wachmann-Kolpe)/ Wenn Ich Mir 'Was Wünschen Dürfte (Holländer)
Side Two: Johnny, Wenn Du Geburtstag Hast (Holländer)/ Marie-Marie (Bécaud-Delanoe)/Lili Marlene (Schultze-Leip)/ Ich Weiss Nicht zu Wem Ich Gehöre (Holländer-Liebmann)/ Ich Hab' Noch einen Koffer in Berlin (Siegel-Pinelli)/ Kinder, Heut' Abend (Holländer)

Matrix numbers: 2 XRA 1116 and 1117; catalogue number: Electrola E 83 220
This LP was also issued in Great Britain as *Marlene Dietrich Returns to Germany*, with the addition of 'Sag Mir Wo die Blumen Sind'. Catalogue number: CLP 1659

London, November 1963 and September 1964

Die Neue Marlene: Marlene Dietrich Sings in German
Side One: Wenn die Soldaten (trad. arr. Pronk)/ Die Antwort Weiss Ganz Allein der Wind (Blowin' in the Wind) (Dylan-Bradtke)/ In den Kasernen (Gerard-Koch)/ Und Wenn Er Wiederkommt (Gerard-Colpet-Maeterlinck)/ Sag Mir Wo die Blumen Sind (Where Have All the Flowers Gone) (Seeger-Colpet)/ Auf der Mundharmonika (Spoliansky-Gilbert)
Side Two: Der Trommelmann (The Little Drummerboy) (Simeone-Onorati-Davis-Buschor)/ Wenn der Sommer Wieder Einzieht (A Little on the Lonely Side) (Cavanaugh-Weldon-Robertson-Metzl)/ Ich Werde Dich Lieben (Theme for Young Lovers) Welch-Dietrich)/ Paff, der Zauberdrachen (Puff the Magic Dragon) (Yarrow-Lipton-Oldörp)/ Ssch, Kleines Baby (Hush Little Baby) (Siegel-Costa-Dietrich)/ Mutter, Hast Du Mir Vergeben (Czy mnie jeszcze pamietasz) (Nieman-Grau-Dietrich)

No orchestra is credited on the label or sleeve of the original issue of this recording, but Burt Bacharach directed the studio orchestra and was responsible for the arrangements of all the songs

Marlene Singt Berlin
Arranged and conducted by Bert Grund; recorded 1964
Side One: Solang Noch Unter'n Linden (Walter Kollo)/ Du Hast Ja Keine Ahnung, Wie Schön Du Bist, Berlin (Jean Gilbert-Schönfeld)/ Durch Berlin Fliesst Immer Noch die Spree (Jean Gilbert-Robert Gilbert)/ Mit Dir, Mit Dir, Da Möcht' Ich Sonntags Angeln Geh'n (Walter Kollo-Rideamus)/ Nach Meine Beene ist Ja Ganz Berlin Verrückt (Walter Kollo-Hardt)/Ja, Das Haben die Mädchen So Gerne (Jean Gilbert-Schönfeld)/ Lieber Leierkastenmann (Willi Kollo)
Side Two: Das War in Schönberg (Walter Kollo-Bernauer Schanzer)/ Unter'n Linden – Unter'n Linden (Walter Kollo-Bernauer Schanzer)/ Das Zille-Lied (Willi Kollo-Pflanzer)/ Wenn Du Einmal eine Braut Hast (Hirsch-Heye)/ Wo Hast Du Nur die Schönen Blauen Augen Her (Erwin-Katscher)/ Berlin-Berlin (Willi Kollo)/ Solang Noch Unter'n Linden (Walter Kollo)

Dietrich in London
Arranged and directed by Burt Bacharach
Side One: I Can't Give You Anything But Love (Fields/McHugh)/ The Laziest Gal in Town (Cole Porter)/ Shir Hatan (Sahar)/ La Vie en Rose (Louiguy-Piaf)/ Johnny (Holländer)/ Go 'Way from My Window (J.J. Niles)/ Allein (Waxman-Colpe)
Side Two: Lili Marlene (Schultze-Leip-Connor)/ Warum (Stolz-Reisch-Robinson)/ Lola (Holländer-Liebmann)/ Marie-Marie (Bécaud)/ Honeysuckle Rose (Waller-Razaf)/ Falling in Love Again (Holländer-Lerner)

Matrix numbers: NN 1113H–A/B; catalogue number: Pye NPL 18113

M.D. Live
Side One: Hot Voodoo (Coslow-Rainger)/ You Little So-and-So (Coslow-Rainger)/ I Couldn't Be Annoyed (Coslow-Rainger)/ Quand l'Amour Meurt (Crémieux)/ Awake in a Dream (Holländer)/ Falling in Love Again (Holländer)/ I've Been in Love Before (Holländer)/ Symphonie (Bernstein)/ La Vie en Rose (Louiguy-Piaf)/ Ein Roman (Kaper)/ Let's Call It a Day (De Sylva-Brown-Henderson)
Side Two: No Love, No Nothin' (Robin-Warren)/ It Must Have Been Something I Dreamt Last Night/ Lieb zu Mir (Mean to Me) (Turk-Alhert-Metzl)/ Das Alte Lied (Love)/ Ich Weiss Nicht, zu Wem Ich Gehöre (Holländer-Liebmann)/ La Vie en Rose (Louiguy-Piaf) (duet with Bing Crosby)/ Je Sais que Vous Êtes Jolie (Poupon-Christiné)/ Frag Nicht Warum (Stolz)/ Love Me

Wildebeest-Maclon Co. Record Maclon 5290; published 1975

Lili Marlene
Side One: Lili Marlene (Schultze)/ Black Market (Holländer)/ Illusions (Holländer)/ The Ruins of Berlin (Holländer)/ The Boys in the Backroom (Holländer)
Side Two: Lola (Holländer)/ Way Back Home in Indiana (Macdonald-Hanley)/ Falling in Love Again (Holländer)/ Blonde Women (Holländer)/ This Evening, Children (Holländer)

Nostalgia LP 22005, Luzern, W. Germany 1984.
These two LPs both contain soundtrack recordings from Dietrich's films, as well as off-the-air American radio recordings from the late 1940s and early 1950s. The somewhat irregular status of the copyright meant that the records had a limited circulation.

Bing's Beaus
Radio broadcasts of Bing Crosby with Marlene Dietrich and Tallulah Bankhead, recorded early 1950s; issued 1980

FILMOGRAPHY

Some sources claim that Dietrich appeared as an extra in German silent films as early as 1920; no evidence of this has yet been produced. Those silent films in which she did appear have been chronicled many times, although few of them have been shown in recent decades. The only one that features regularly on the programmes of film museums and societies – Pabst's *Die Freudlose Gasse* – contains in its surviving prints only a very brief scene in which Dietrich is recognizable. 'They're not important' and 'I didn't make any films before *The Blue Angel*' have been Dietrich's standard responses to any questions about her silent films. 'I just had a few "little moments",' she told Maximilian Schell. In deference to her views, these films are merely listed here. The Dietrich style we know and love only really emerged in April 1930, when *The Blue Angel* received its world première in Berlin.

Silent Films

Der Kleine Napoleon, 1923. Directed by Georg Jacoby
Tragödie der Liebe, 1923. Directed by Joe May
Der Mensch am Wege, 1923. Directed by Wilhelm Dieterle
Der Sprung ins Leben, 1924. Directed by Johannes Guter
Die Freudlose Gasse, 1925. Directed by Georg Wilhelm Pabst
Manon Lescaut, 1926. Directed by Arthur Robinson
Eine Dubarry von Heute, 1926. Directed by Alexander Korda
Madame Wünschte Keine Kinder, 1926. Directed by Alexander Korda
Kopf Hoch, Charly!, 1926. Directed by Willi Wolff
Der Juxbaron, 1927. Directed by Willi Wolff
Sein Grösster Bluff, 1927. Directed by Harry Piel
Café Electric, 1927. Directed by Gustav Ucicky
Prinzessin Olala, 1928. Directed by Robert Land
Ich Küsse Ihre Hand, Madame, 1929. Directed by Robert Land
Die Frau, Nach der Man Sich Sehnt, 1929. Directed by Kurt Bernhardt
Das Schiff der Verlorenen Menschen, 1929. Directed by Maurice Tourneur
Gefahren der Brautzeit, 1929. Directed by Fred Sauer

Feature Films

Der Blaue Engel (The Blue Angel), Germany 1930. Directed by Josef von Sternberg; produced by Erich Pommer; script by Robert Liebmann, based on Heinrich Mann's novel *Professor Unrath*; photography by Gunther Rittau, Hans Schneeberger; design by Otto Hunte, Emil Hasler; music by Friedrich Holländer. With Hans Albers, Kurt Gerron, Emil Jannings and Rosa Valetti.

Morocco, USA 1930. Directed by Josef von Sternberg; script by Jules Furthman, based on Benno Vigny's play *Amy Jolly*; photography by Lee Garmes; design by Hans Dreier, Travis Banton; music by Leo Robin, Karl Hajos, Crémieux. With Gary Cooper, Ullrich Haupt and Adolphe Menjou.

Dishonored (X 27), USA 1931. Directed by Josef von Sternberg; script by Daniel H. Rubin, based on a story by Josef von Sternberg; photography by Lee Garmes; design by Travis Banton; music by Karl Hajos. With Victor McLaglen and Gustav von Seyffertitz.

Shanghai Express, USA 1932. Directed by Josef von Sternberg; script by Jules Furthman; photography by Lee Garmes; design by Hans Dreier, Travis Banton; music by W. Franke Harling. With Clive Brook, Warner Oland and Anna May Wong.

Blonde Venus, USA 1932. Directed by Josef von Sternberg; script by Jules Furthman and S.K. Lauren, based on a story by Josef von Sternberg; photography by Bert Glennon; design by Wiard Ihnen, Travis Banton; music by Oscar Potoker, Sam Coslow, Ralph Rainger, Dick Whiting. With Cary Grant, Herbert Marshall and Dickie Moore.

Song of Songs, USA, Paramount, 1933. Directed by Rouben Mamoulian; script by Leo Birinski, Samuel Hoffenstein, based on the novel by Hermann Sudermann and the play by Edward Sheldon; photography by Victor Milner; design by Travis Banton; music by Karl Hajos, Milan Roder, Friedrich Holländer. With Brian Aherne, Lionel Atwill and Alison Skipworth.

The Scarlet Empress, USA, Paramount, 1934. Directed by Josef von Sternberg, Manuel Komroff; photography by Bert Glennon; design by Hans Dreier, Peter Ballbusch, Richard Kollorsz, Travis Banton; music by W. Franke Harling, John M. Leipold, Milan Roder. With John Lodge, Sam Jaffe, Louise Dresser and Maria Sieber.

The Devil is a Woman, USA, Paramount, 1935. Directed by Josef von Sternberg; script by John Dos Passos, S.K. Winston, based on Pierre Louys's novel *La Femme et le Pantin*; photography by Lucien Ballard; design by Hans Dreier, Travis Banton; music by Rimski-Korsakov, Leo Robin, Ralph Rainger. With Lionel Atwill, Cesar Romero and Alison Skipworth.

Desire, USA, Paramount, 1936. Directed by Frank Borzage; produced by Ernst Lubitsch; script by Edwin Justis Mayer, Waldemar Young, Samuel Hoffenstein; photography by Charles Lang; design by Hans Dreier, Robert Usher, Travis Banton; music by Friedrich Holländer. With Gary Cooper, John Halliday and Zeffie Tilbury.

I Loved a Soldier (incomplete, lost), USA, Paramount, 1936. Directed by Henry Hathaway; produced by Benjamin Glazer; script by John van Druten, based on Melchior Lengyel's book *Hotel Stadt Lemberg*. With Charles Boyer.

The Garden of Allah, USA, Selznick International, 1936. Directed by Richard Boleslawski; produced by David O. Selznick; script by W.P. Lipscomb, Lynn Riggs, based on the play and novel by Robert Hichens; photography by W. Howard Greene; design by Sturges Carne, Lyle Wheeler, Edward Boyle, Ernst Dryden; music by Max Steiner. With Charles Boyer, Basil Rathbone, Joseph Schildkraut and Tilly Losch.

Knight without Armour, UK, London Films, 1937. Directed by Jacques Feyder; produced by Alexander Korda; script by Lajos Biro, Arthur Wimperis, Frances Marion, based on James Hilton's novel; photography by Harry Stradling; design by Lazare Meerson, George Benda; music by Miklos Rosza. With Robert Donat, Basil Gill and Robert Clements.

Angel, USA, Paramount, 1937. Directed by Ernst Lubitsch; script by Samson Raphaelson, based on the play by Melchior Lengyel adapted by Guy Bolton and Russell Medcraft; photography by Charles Lang; design by Hans Dreier, Robert Usher, Travis Banton; music by Friedrich Holländer. With Herbert Marshall and Melvyn Douglas.

Destry Rides Again, USA, Universal, 1939. Directed by George Marshall; produced by Joe Pasternak; script by Felix Jackson, Henry Meyers and Gertrude Purcell, based on the novel by Max Brand; photography by Hal Mohr; design by Jack Otterson, Vera West; music by Friedrich Holländer. With James Stewart, Charles Winninger, Mischa Auer, Una Merkel and Brian Donlevy.

Seven Sinners, USA, Universal, 1940. Directed by Tay Garnett; produced by Joe Pasternak; script by John Meehan, Harry Tugend, based on the story by Ladislaus Fodor, Lazlo Vadnal; photography by Rudolph Mate; design by Jack Otterson, Irene (Dietrich's costumes); music by Friedrich Holländer. With John Wayne, Broderick Crawford, Mischa Auer and Anna Lee.

The Flame of New Orleans, USA, Universal, 1941. Directed by René Clair; produced by Joe Pasternak; script by Norman Krasna; photography by Rudolph Mate; design by Jack Otterson, Martin Obzina, Russell A. Gausman, René Hubert; music by Charles Previn. With Bruce Cabot, Roland Young and Theresa Harris.

Manpower, USA, Warner Brothers – First National, 1941. Directed by Raoul Walsh; produced by Mark Hellinger; script by Richard Macauley, Jerry Wald; photography by Ernest Haller; design by Max Parker, Milo Anderson; music by Adolph Deutsch, Friedrich Holländer. With Edward G. Robinson and George Raft.

The Lady is Willing, USA, Columbia, 1942. Directed by Mitchell Leisen; script by James Edward Grant, Albert McCleery; photography by Ted Teizlaff; design by Rudolph Sternad, Irene; music by Morris Stoloff. With Fred MacMurray, Aline McMahon and Davy Joseph James.

The Spoilers, USA, Universal, 1942. Directed by Ray Enright; produced by Frank Lloyd; script by Lawrence Hazard, Tom Reed, based on the novel by Rex Beech; photography by Milton Krasner; design by Jack Otterson, John B. Goodman, Vera West; music by Hans J. Salter, Charles Previn. With John Wayne, Randolph Scott and Marietta Canty.

Pittsburgh, USA, Universal, 1942. Directed by Lewis Seiler; produced by Charles K. Feldman; script by Kenneth Gamet, Tom Reed, based on a story by George Owen and Tom Reed; photography by Robert de Grasse; design by John B. Goodman, Russell A. Gausman, Ira S. Webb, Vera West; music by Charles Previn. With John Wayne and Randolph Scott.

Kismet, USA, MGM, 1944. Directed by William Dieterle; produced by Everett Riskin; script by John Meehan, based on the play by Edward Knobloch; photography by Charles Rosher; design by Cedric Gibbons, Daniel B. Cathcart, Irene; music by Herbert Stothart, Harold Arlen, E.Y. Harburg. With Ronald Colman, Edward Arnold and Joy Ann Page.

Martin Roumagnac, France, Alcina Production, 1946. Directed by Georges Lacombe; produced by Marc Le Pelletier; script by Pierre Very, based on the novel by Pierre-René Wolf; photography by Roger Hubert; design by Georges Wakhevitch; music by Marcel Mirouze. With Jean Gabin, Margo Lion and Daniel Gelin.

Golden Earrings, USA, Paramount, 1947. Directed by Mitchell Leisen; produced by Harry Tugend; script by Frank Butler and Helen Deutsch, based on the novel by Yolanda Foldes; photography by Daniel L. Fapp; design by Hans Dreier, John Meehan; music by Victor Young. With Ray Milland and Bruce Lester.

A Foreign Affair, USA, Paramount, 1948. Directed by Billy Wilder; produced by Charles Brackett; script by Billy Wilder, Charles Brackett, Richard L. Breen; photography by Charles B. Lang Jr; design by Edith Head; music by Friedrich Holländer. With Jean Arthur, John Lund and Millard Mitchell.

Stage Fright, UK, Warner Brothers–First National, 1950. Directed by Alfred Hitchcock; script by Whitfield Cook, based on the novel *Man Running* by Selwyn Jepson; photography by Wilkie Cooper; design by Terence Verity (Dietrich's gowns by Christian Dior); music by Leighton Lucas, Cole Porter. With Alistair Sim, Richard Todd and Jane Wyman.

No Highway, UK, Twentieth Century-Fox, 1951. Directed by Henry Koster; produced by Louis D. Lighton; script by R.C. Sherriff, Oscar Millard and Alec Coppel, based on the novel by Nevil Shute; photography by Georges Perinal; design by C.P. Norman (Dietrich's gowns by Christian Dior and Pierre Balmain). With James Stewart, Glynis Johns and Jack Hawkins.

Rancho Notorious, USA, RKO-Radio, 1952. Directed by Fritz Lang; produced by Howard Welsch; script by Daniel Taradash, based on a story by Sylvia Richards; photography by Hal Mohr; design by Robert Priestley (Dietrich's gowns by Don Loper); music by Emil Newman, Ken Darby. With Arthur Kennedy and Mel Ferrer.

The Monte Carlo Story, Italy, United Artists, 1957. Directed by Samuel A. Taylor; produced by Marcello Girosi; script by Samuel Taylor; photography by Giuseppe Rotunno; design by Gastone Medin (Dietrich's gowns by Jean Louis); music by Michel Emer. With Vittorio de Sica and Mischa Auer.

Witness for the Prosecution, USA, United Artists, 1958. Directed by Billy Wilder; produced by Arthur Hornblow Jr; script by Billy Wilder and Harry Kurnitz, based on the play by Agatha Christie; photography by Russell Harlan; design by Howard Bristol (Dietrich's gowns by Edith Head); music by Matty Melneck, Ralph Arthur Roberts, Jack Brooks. With Tyrone Power, Charles Laughton and Elsa Lanchester.

Touch of Evil, USA, Universal-International, 1958. Directed by Orson Welles; produced by Albert Zugsmith; script by Orson Welles, based on the novel *Badge of Evil* by Whit Masterson; photography by Russell Metty; design by Bill Thomas; music by Henry Mancini. With Orson Welles, Charlton Heston and Janet Leigh.

Judgment at Nuremberg, USA, United Artists, 1961. Directed by Stanley Kramer; produced by Stanley Kramer, Philip Langner; script by Abby Mann; photography by Ernest Laszlio; design by Rudolph Sternad; music by Ernest Gold. With Spencer Tracy, Maximilian Schell, Burt Lancaster, Judy Garland, Richard Widmark and Montgomery Clift.

The Black Fox, USA, Heritage Films, 1962. Directed by Louis Clyde Stoumen; produced by Jack Le Vien; script by Louis Clyde Stoumen; music by Ezra Laderman. Dietrich was the narrator.

Just a Gigolo, UK-Germany, Leguan, 1978. Directed by David Hemmings; produced by Rolf Thiele; script by Ennio de Concini; photography by Charly Steinberger; design by Peter Rothe; music by Günther Fischer, L. Casucci, Irving Caesar. With David Bowie, Kim Novak, Maria Schell, David Hemmings and Curt Jurgens.

Marlene, Germany, Zev Braun Pictures, 1984. Directed by Maximilian Schell; produced by Peter Genee; photography by Ivan Slapeta; music by Nicholas Economou. With Maximilian Schell and Annie Albers.

Guest Appearances
Dietrich made guest appearances in four films which – to her annoyance – are often listed as 'her films'. They are: *Follow the Boys* (USA, 1944. Directed by Eddie Sutherland, with Orson Welles); *Jigsaw* (USA, 1949. Directed by Fletcher Markle, with Henry Fonda); *Around the World in 80 Days* (USA, 1956. Directed by Michael Anderson, with Frank Sinatra); and *Paris When It Sizzles* (USA, 1964. Directed by Richard Quine, with costumes by Dior).

Bibliography

Kenneth Anger, *Hollywood Babylon* (APS Inc., Phoenix, 1965)
Jean-Pierre Aumont, *Le Soleil et les Ombres* (Robert Laffont, Paris, 1976)
Cecil Beaton, *Cecil Beaton's Scrapbook* (Batsford, London, 1937)
    Photobiography (Odhams, London, 1951)
    The Parting Years (Weidenfeld, London, 1978)
Chantal Brunschwig, et al., *100 Ans de Chanson Français* (Seuil, Paris, 1972)
Larry Carr, *Four Fabulous Faces* (Galahad Books, New York, 1970)
Jean Cocteau, *Lettres à Jean Marais* (Albin Michel, Paris, 1987)
    Past Tense: The Cocteau Diaries Volume Two, translated by Richard Howard (Harcourt, Brace, Jovanovich, New York, 1988)
Terry Comito, *Touch of Evil, Orson Welles, Director* (Rutgers University Press, New Brunswick, 1987)
Jacques Damase, *Les Folies du Music-Hall* (Anthony Blond, London, 1962)
Bette Davis, *The Lonely Life* (Macdonald, London, 1962)
Thierry De Navacelle, *Sublime Marlene*, translated by C.L. Smith (Sidgwick & Jackson, London, 1984)
Homer Dickens, *The Films of Marlene Dietrich* (Citadel Press, New York, 1968)
Marlene Dietrich, *Nehmt Nur Mein Leben* (Bertelsmann/Goldman, Munich, 1979)
    Marlene D., translated by Boris Mattews (Grasset, Paris, 1984)
    My Life, translated by Salvator Attanasio (Weidenfeld, London, 1989)
    Marlene Dietrich's ABC, revised edition (Ungar, New York, 1984). First published 1961.
    Vogue par Marlene Dietrich (Éditions Condé Nast, Paris, December 1973)
David Drew, *Kurt Weill – A Handbook* (Faber, London, 1987)
René Droz, *Marlene Dietrich und die Psychologie des Vamps* (Sanssouci Verlag, Zurich, 1961)
Susan Everett, *Lost Berlin* (Gallery Books, New York, 1979)
Leslie Frewin, *Blond Venus: A Life of Marlene Dietrich* (MacGibbon & Kee, London, 1955)
Curtis Harrington, *An Index to the Films of Josef von Sternberg* (special supplement to *Sight and Sound*, London, 1949)
Charles Higham, *Marlene* (Granada, London, 1977)
A.E. Hotchner, *Papa Hemingway* (Weidenfeld, London, 1967)
Brigid Keenan, *Dior in Vogue* (Octopus Books, London, 1981)
John Kobal, *Marlene Dietrich* (Studio Vista, London, 1968)
    People Will Talk (Aurum Press, London, 1988)
Gavin Lambert, *On Cukor* (W.H. Allen, London, 1972)
Elizabeth Leese, *Costume Design in the Movies* (BCW Publishing, Isle of Wight, 1976)
Berthold Leimbach, *Tondokumente der Kleinkunst und ihre Interpreten 1898–1945* (Göttingen, 1991)
Abby Mann, *Judgment at Nuremberg* (Cassel, London, 1961)
Sheridan Morley, *Marlene Dietrich* (Elm Tree Books, London, 1976)
Wolfgang Noa, *Marlene Dietrich* (Henschelverlag, Berlin, 1964)
Barry Paris, *Louise Brooks* (Hamish Hamilton, London, 1989)
Graham Payn and Sheridan Morley, *The Noël Coward Diaries* (Weidenfeld, London, 1982)
'PEM', *Und der Himmel Hängt Voller Geigen* (Lothar Blanvalet, Berlin, 1955)
Paul Rose, *Berlins grosse Theaterzeit* (Rembrandt, Berlin, 1969)

Brian Rust, *The Complete Entertainment Discography 1890–1942* (Da Capo Press, New York, 1989)
Ronald Sanders, *The Days Grow Short – The Life and Music of Kurt Weill* (Holt, Rinehart and Winston, New York, 1980)
Andrew Sarris, *The Films of Josef von Sternberg* (Museum of Modern Art, New York, 1966)
Arthur M. Schlesinger Jr, *Robert Kennedy and His Times* (André Deutsch, London, 1978)
Otto Schneidereit, *Berlin wie es Weint und Lacht* (VEB Lied der Zeit, Berlin, 1968)
Klaus-Jürgen Sembach, *Marlene Dietrich* (Schirmer-Mosel, Munich, 1984)
Ginette Spanier, *It Isn't All Mink* (Collins, London, 1959)
Habakuk Traber and Elmar Weingarten, *Verdrängte Musik – Berliner Komponisten im Exil* (Argon, Berlin, 1987)
Richard Traubner, *Operetta – A Theatrical History* (Gollancz, London, 1984)
Kathleen Tynan, *Kenneth Tynan* (Methuen, London, 1988)
Kenneth Tynan and Cecil Beaton, *Persona Grata* (Wingate, London, 1953)
Bruno Villien, *Hitchcock* (Éditions Colona, Paris, 1982)
Josef von Sternberg, *Fun in a Chinese Laundry* (Secker & Warburg, London, 1965)
    The Blue Angel (Lorrimer, London, 1968)
    Morocco and Shanghai Express (Simon & Schuster, New York, 1973)
Alexander Walker, *Dietrich* (Thames & Hudson, London, 1984)
Francis Wyndham, *The Theatre of Embarrassment* (Chatto, London, 1991)
John Willett, *The Theatre of the Weimar Republic* (Holmes & Meier, New York, 1988)
Carole Zucker, *The Idea of the Image – Josef von Sternberg's Dietrich Films* (Associated University Presses, Cranbury, New Jersey, 1988)

NEWSPAPER AND MAGAZINE ARTICLES

Since 1930 hardly a week has passed without someone writing an article about Dietrich. It would take a separate book to attempt to list them, but among those articles I have found most illuminating are:

Peter Bogdanovich, 'Josef von Sternberg' (*Movie*, no. 13, summer 1965)
Alain Bosquet, 'Marlène Dietrich Raconte l'Ange Bleu' (*Le Figaro*, 17 April 1991)
David Colby, 'The Dietrich Tapes' (*The Manipulator*, no. 2, 1984)
Serge Daney and Jean-Louis Noames, 'Rencontres avec un Solitaire' (*Cahiers du Cinéma*, July 1965)
Cynthia Kee, 'Me and My Clothes' (interview with Marlene Dietrich in the *Observer*, 6 March 1960)
Sheridan Morley, 'Dietrich at 70 – or Thereabouts' (*The Times*, 11 June 1973)
Derek Prouse, 'Dietrich: I Hated Being a Film Star' (The *Sunday Times*, 22 November 1964)
David Robinson, 'Dietrich Before *The Blue Angel*' (*The Times*, 14 July 1977)
Deborah Thomas, 'Blonde Venus' (*Movie* no. 34/35, winter 1990)
Josef von Sternberg, 'A Taste for Celluloid' (*Films and Filming*, July 1963)
Richard Whitehall, 'The Blue Angel' (*Films and Filming*, October 1962)

You'll try in vain
You can't explain
The charming, alarming
Blonde women

ACKNOWLEDGEMENTS

I am grateful to the following individuals and organizations for permission to quote from published texts: the literary executors for the late Sir Cecil Beaton for extracts from *Cecil Beaton's Scrapbook* and *Photobiography*; Michael Imison Playwrights for the extract from Noël Coward's verse, © the Estate of Noël Coward; the Society of Authors and the Estate of George Bernard Shaw for the extracts from *Misalliance* © 1914; Kathleen Tynan and the literary executors of the late Kenneth Tynan for an extract from *One or Two Things I Know of Her* and other writings; Francis Wyndham and Chatto & Windus for an extract from *The Theatre of Embarrassment*. The lyrics of 'Falling in Love Again' and 'Blonde Women' are by Sam Winston © 1930; 'The World Was Young' is by Philippe-Gérard-Vannier-Mercer © Macmelodies, Britico. For details of other lyrics quoted, see the bibliography.

Many other people and organizations have been of valuable assistance to me in the course of writing about Dietrich. I would particularly like to thank the curators and staff of the National Film Archive in London, who over the years have answered hundreds of questions and put their unique collection at my disposal; the Theatre Museum of the Victoria and Albert Museum; the library staff at the British Library, National Sound Archive; and the curators and staff of the theatre collection at the Performing Arts Research Center of New York Public Library at Lincoln Center, who have always offered most courteous, efficient and patient help. Of the friends who have provided willing help and opinions – and who have come with me over the years to see Dietrich's films and to hear her sing – I especially want to thank David Cronin, Peter Eyre, Francis Wyndham, Bruno Villien, Oliver Smith, John Culme, Patrick Libby, Jonathan Gili, James Jolly, Tim de Lisle and Tim Rostron.

At Bloomsbury Publishing, Liz Calder, Rachel King, Penny Phillips and David Reynolds have supervised the production of the book at breakneck speed, and Graham Curd, Laurence Bradbury and Roy Williams have masterminded the *mise-en-page* in the grand tradition.

My greatest thanks go, of course, to Marlene Dietrich herself who, although she had nothing to do with the conception of the book, has entertained the twentieth century with her own, amazing, style.